THE

DHARMA FLOWER

SUTRA

THE WONDERFUL DHARMA LOTUS FLOWER SUTRA

Translated into English by
Tripitaka Master Kumarajiva of Yao Ch'in

Volume 6,
Chapter 5, Medicinal Herbs
Chapter 6, Conferring Predictions

with the commentary of
TRIPITAKA
MASTER HUA

Translated into English by
The Buddhist Text Translation Society
San Francisco
1980

Translated by the Buddhist Text Translation Society
Primary translation: Bhikshuni Heng-yin
Reviewed by: Bhikshuni Heng-ch'ih
Edited by: Upasika Kuo-lin Lethcoe

Certified by: The Venerable Master Hua

Printed in the United States of America

First printing--1980

For information address:
    Sino American Buddhist Association
    Dharma Realm Buddhist University
    Gold Mountain Monastery
    1731 15th Street
    San Francisco, California 94103
    U.S.A.
    (415) 621-5202
    (415) 861-9672

ISBN 0-917512-65-0

Acknowledgements:

Cover: Bhikshuni Heng-chieh
Index: Bhikshuni Heng-ming
English calligraphy (Sutra text and other) Jerri-jo
Illuminated letters: Kuo-ling Pecaites
Graphics and layout: Jerri-jo Idarius and
    Kuo-ling Pecaites
Photo of the Master: Kuo-ying Brevoort.
Commentary typed by: Upasika Kuo-shan

The Venerable Master Hua

Introduction

The present volume contains Chapters Five and Six of The Wonderful Dharma Lotus Flower Sutra. In Chapter Five: Medicinal Herbs, the Buddha's speaking of Dharma is likened to the rain falling from a great cloud. The rain falls equally on all the different grasses and trees, and they each absorb as much of the moisture as they are able. Likewise, the Thus Come One speaks the Dharma of a single flavor, a single mark, the mark of liberation and extinction. Living beings receive it differently according to their individual dispositions and natures. Moistened by the Dharma rain, their good roots grow, and, eventually they realize Buddhahood.

In Chapter Six: Conferring Predictions, the Buddha bestows predictions upon four of his disciples: Mahakasyapa, Subhuti, Mahakatyayana, and Mahamaudgalyayana. In bestowing predictions to those of average dispositions, the Buddha narrates their causal practice, tells of their attainment of the fruit, the name of their future Buddhaland, lifespan as a Buddha, and the length of the proper and image Dharma ages.

Table of Contents

CHAPTER FIVE: OUTLINE

F3. Thus Come One's narration. (1036)
Gl. General narration.(1036)
  H1. Doubly praising Kashyapa, "Good indeed!" (1036)
  H2. Inability to speak fully of Buddha's virtues. (1037)
G2. Expanded narration. (1037)
  H1. Prose. (1037)
    I1. Showing the inconceivability of Provisional and Real. (1037)
      J1. Speaking Dharma. (1038)
        K1. Showing Provisional and Real Teachings as inconceivable. (1038)
        K2. Showing Provisional and Real Wisdom as inconceivable. (1039)
      J2. Setting up analogy. (1040)
        K1. Analogy of just the Real is the Provisional-- not different and yet different. (1041)
          L1.Showing that which can produce and that which is produced, although not different, are different. (1041)
          L2. That which is moistened and that which moistens although not different, are different.(1043)
        K2. Analogy of just the Provisional is the Real-- different and yet not different. (1043)
      J3. Correlation with Dharma. (1045)
        K1. Corr. of "not different and yet different." (1045)
          L1. Corr. proper. (1045)
            M1. First corr. "that which moistens." (1046)
            M2. Corr. that which is produced with that which produces. (1050)

CHAPTER SIX: OUTLINE

Chapter Five: Medicinal Herbs

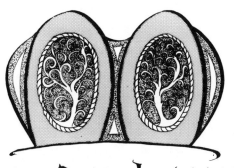 ĒĐICIN∂L ḣ∂RBS∂RĒ USĒĐ ⊂O ḣ∂∂L ICCNĒSSĒS.

This, the Fifth Chapter of <u>The Wonderful Dharma Lotus Flower Sutra</u>, uses the herbs as an analogy. Medicinal herbs can cure sickness, but they have to be administered properly. If they are administered incorrectly, not only will they fail to cure the sickness, they will make it worse.

Sutra: T262 19a 17

At that time the World Honored One told Mahakashyapa and all the great disciples, "Good indeed! Good indeed! Kashyapa has well spoken of the Thus Come One's real and true merit and virtue. It is just as he said.

Outline:

F3. Thus Come One's narration.

G1. General narration.

H1. Doubly praising Kashyapa, "Good indeed, good indeed!"

AT THAT TIME, right after Mahakashyapa had praised the Buddhadharma in verse, THE WORLD HONORED ONE, Shakyamuni Buddha, TOLD MAHAKASHYAPA AND ALL THE GREAT DISCIPLES assembled there, "GOOD INDEED! GOOD INDEED! You are really good, really good. KASHYAPA HAS WELL SPOKEN OF THE THUS COME ONE'S REAL MERIT AND VIRTUE. IT IS JUST AS YOU SAID. You have spoken very correctly. However...

Sutra: T 19a 19

Furthermore, the Thus Come One has limitless, boundless asankheyas of merit and virtue. If you were to speak of it throughout limitless millions of aeons, you could not finish.

Outline:

> H2. Inability to speak fully
>
> of Buddha's virtues.

Commentary:

"FURTHERMORE, THE THUS COME ONE HAS LIMITLESS, uncountable, BOUNDLESS ASANKHEYAS, an uncountable number OF MERIT AND VIRTUE. The merit and virtue he has cultivated and practiced. IF YOU WERE TO SPEAK OF THEM THROUGHOUT LIMITLESS MILLIONS OF AEONS, YOU COULD NOT FINISH. If you spoke all day long, day after day, throughout an unreckonable amount of time, you still couldn't finish.

Sutra: T 19a 22

Kashyapa, you should know that the Thus Come One is the king of all the dharmas. Nothing that he teaches is false. He extensively proclaims all dharmas by means of wisdom and expedients, and whatever dharmas he speaks all lead to the ground of all wisdom.

Outline:

> G2. Expanded narration.
>
> H1. Prose
>
> > I1. Showing the inconceivability of Provisional and Real.

J1. Speaking Dharma.

K1. Showing Pro-
visional and Real
Teachings as in-
conceivable.

Commentary:

"KASHYAPA, YOU SHOULD KNOW THAT THE THUS COME ONE IS
THE KING OF ALL THE DHARMAS." All dharmas are born from
the Buddha. "NOTHING THAT HE SAYS IS FALSE everything he
says is true. HE PROCLAIMS ALL DHARMAS BY MEANS OF WIS-
DOM AND EXPEDIENTS. In his teaching he includes the dharmas of all Three Vehicles. Wisely he employs clever expedients to proclaim all the dharmas. AND WHATEVER DHARMAS
HE SPEAKS ALL LEAD TO THE GROUND OF ALL WISDOM." The
Dharmas the Thus Come One teaches lead to the other shore
of wisdom. All wisdom is one of the three types of wisdom
the Thus Come One possesses: the wisdom of all modes, the
wisdom of the Way, and all-wisdom. (cf. Vol. 2, p.302)

Sutra: T 19 a 25
*The Thus Come One contemplates and
knows the tendencies of all dharmas. He also
knows the depths of the mental processes of
all living beings, having penetrated them without obstruction. Furthermore, he has ultimate*

and clear understanding of all dharmas, and he instructs living beings in all-wisdom.

K2. Showing Provi-
sional and Real
Wisdom as incon-
ceivable.

Commentary:

THE THUS COME ONE, the Buddha, has three bodies and four wisdoms, five eyes and six spiritual penetrations.

The Three Bodies are: the Dharma Body, the Reward Body, and the Transformation Body. The Four Wisdoms are: the Great Perfect Mirror Wisdom, the Equality Nature Wisdom, the Wonderful Observing Wisdom, and the Perfecting Wisdom.

The Five Eyes are: the Buddha-eye, the Dharma-eye, the Heavenly-eye, the Wisdom-eye, and the Flesh-eye.

The Six Spiritual Penetrations are: the Penetration of the Heavenly Eye, the Penetration of the Heavenly Ear, the Penetration of Other's Thoughts, the Penetration of the Knowledge of Past Lives, the Penetration of the Extinction of Outflows, and the Penetration of the Complete Spirit. With such wisdom, he CONTEMPLATES AND KNOWS all dharmas. There are 84,000 dharmas. If one were to list them all separately, it would take way too much time, so the text simply says, THE TENDENCIES OF ALL DHARMAS. And just where do all dharmas tend? All dharmas are not apart

from the minds of living beings. All dharmas arise mani-
fested only through the mind. All dharmas manifest through
the mind, and they return--they "tend"--towards the mind.
HE ALSO KNOWS THE DEPTHS OF THE MENTAL PROCESSES OF
ALL LIVING BEINGS. Every thought they have, the Buddha
knows. That is why The Vajra Sutra says, "The Thus Come
One knows the thoughts in the minds of all living beings."
HAVING PENETRATED THEM WITHOUT OBSTRUCTION. He under-
stands what living beings are thinking, totally. FURTHER-
MORE, HE HAS ULTIMATE AND CLEAR UNDERSTANDING OF ALL DHAR-
MAS. He has fathomed all dharmas completely; he completely
understands them, and so HE INSTRUCTS LIVING BEINGS IN ALL-
WISDOM. He leads all living beings to attain all-wisdom,
as well.

Sutra: T 19a27

*Kashyapa, consider the world of three thou-
sand great thousand worlds and the grasses,
trees, forests, as well as the medicinal herbs, in
their many varieties, with their different names
and colors which the mountains, streams, valleys
and flatlands produce.*

Outline:

J2. Setting up analogy.

K1. Analogy of just
the Real is the Provi-
sional--not different
yet different.

L1. Showing that
which can produce
and that which is
produced, although
not different, are
different.

Commentary:

"KASHYAPA, I shall now speak to you a parable: CONSID-
ER THE WORLD OF THREE THOUSAND GREAT THOUSAND WORLDS.
One world consists of;

one sun

one moon

one Mount Sumeru

one set of Four Continents

One thousand of these worlds makes up a "small world system." One thousand small world systems makes up a "middle-sized world system." One thousand middle-sized world
systems makes up a "great thousand world system." Because the word "thousand" is used three times, it is called
"the world of three thousand great thousand worlds."

"...AND THE GRASSES, TREES, FORESTS, AS WELL AS MEDIC-
INAL HERBS, IN THEIR MANY VARIETIES. There are many var-

ieties of plants and trees and herbs. WITH THEIR DIFFERENT
NAMES AND COLORS WHICH THE MOUNTAINS, the mountains repre-
sent the great Bodhisattvas, STREAMS, VALLEYS, AND FLAT-
LANDS PRODUCE.

Sutra: T.19a29

A thick cloud spreads out, covering the three thousand great thousand worlds, raining on them equally everywhere at the same time, its moisture reaching every part. The grasses, trees, forests and medicinal herbs – those of small roots, small stalks, small branches and small leaves, those of medium-sized roots, medium-sized stalks, medium-sized branches, medium-sized leaves or those of large roots, large stalks, large branches, and large leaves, and also all the trees, whether great or small, according to their size, small, medium, or large, all receive a portion of it. From the rain of the one cloud each according to its nature grows, blossoms, and bears fruit.

Outline:

L2. That which is
moistened and that

which moistens, al-
though not different,
are different.

Commentary:

"A THICK CLOUD SPREADS OUT, a large, dense cloud
spreads out, COVERING THE THREE THOUSAND GREAT THOUSAND
WORLDS, RAINING ON THEM EQUALLY EVERYWHERE AT THE SAME
TIME, ITS MOISTURE REACHING EVERY PART. It doesn't make
discriminations. THE GRASSES, TREES, FORESTS, AND MEDIC-
INAL HERBS--THOSE OF SMALL ROOTS, SMALL STALKS, SMALL BRANCH-
ES, AND SMALL LEAVES. This represents those of the Small
Vehicle. THOSE OF MEDIUM-SIZED ROOTS, MEDIUM-SIZED BRANCH-
ES, AND MEDIUM-SIZED LEAVES, those of the Middle Vehicle,
THOSE OF LARGE ROOTS, LARGE STALKS, LARGE BRANCHES, those
of the Great Vehicle.

"...AND ALSO ALL THE TREES, WHETHER GREAT OR SMALL, AC-
CORDING TO THEIR SIZE, SMALL, MEDIUM, OR LARGE, ALL RECEIVE
A PORTION OF IT. FROM THE RAIN OF THE ONE CLOUD, EACH GROWS,
BLOSSOMS AND BEARS FRUIT ACCORDING TO ITS NATURE. The small-
er ones receive a smaller amount. The middle-sized ones
get a medium amount, and the large ones get a lot of rain.

Outline:

K2. Analogy of
just the Provi-
sional is the Real

--different and yet

not different.

Sutra: T 19b5

Although they grow from the same ground and are moistened by the same rain, still, all the grasses and trees are different.

Commentary:

"ALTHOUGH THEY GROW FROM THE SAME GROUND AND ARE MOISTENED BY THE SAME RAIN. The Buddha speaks one Dharma, but according to their dispositions, beings absorb what they can of it. STILL, ALL THE GRASSES AND TREES ARE DIFFERENT. The One Vehicle is proclaimed with a single sound, and as the teachings of the Five Vehicles, is received according to the good roots of beings.

Sutra: T 19b6

Kashyapa, you should know that the Thus Come One is also like this. He manifests in the world like a great cloud rising; with his great sound he covers the world with its gods, humans, and asuras, just like that great cloud covers the three thousand great thousand lands. In the midst of the great assembly he announces, "I am the Thus Come One, one worthy of offerings, one of proper and universal knowledge, one whose understanding and conduct are complete, well gone one who understands the world, an unsurpassed lord, a taming and regulating hero, teacher of gods and humans, the Buddha, the World Honored One. Those who have not yet been crossed over, I cross over. Those who have not yet been liberated, I liberate. Those who have not yet been put at rest, I put at rest. Those who have not yet attained Nirvana, I cause to attain Nirvana. I know things as they really are, both in the present and in the future. I am the all-knowing one, the all-seeing one, the one who knows the Way, the one who opens the Way, the one who proclaims the Way. The entire assembly of gods, humans and asuras, all should come here to listen to the Dharma."

Outline:

J3. Correlation with Dharma.

K1. Correlation of not different and yet different.

L1. Correlation proper.

1046

                                    M1. First corre-

                                    lating "that which

                                    moistens."

Commentary:

"KASHYAPA, YOU SHOULD KNOW THE THUS COME ONE, the
World Honored One, IS ALSO LIKE THIS. HE MANIFESTS IN THE
WORLD LIKE A GREAT CLOUD RISING, for the sake of One Matter he manifests in the world to teach and transform living beings, WITH HIS GREAT SOUND HE COVERS THE WORLD WITH
ITS GODS, HUMANS AND ASURAS, JUST LIKE THAT GREAT CLOUD
COVERS THE THREE THOUSAND GREAT THOUSAND LANDS." "Asura"
is a Sanskrit word. It means "no wine," or "ugly." That's
because asuras have the blessings of the heavens, but not
the virtue, and they like to fight. Thieves, for example,
are asuras, yin asuras. Soldiers are yang asuras. There
are asuras in the three good paths, as well as asuras in
the three evil paths, depending on whether they do good
or evil. "IN THE MIDST OF THE GREAT ASSEMBLY HE ANNOUNCES,
'I AM THE THUS COME ONE...'" Someone here is thinking,
"Ah hah! the Buddha must have a concept of a 'self.' He
is saying, 'I am the Thus Come One.'" If you really understand, the Thus Come One has no concept of self at all.
The Buddha has mounted the Way which is thus and comes to
realize right enlightenment.

     I will now give you an example. You are all here
listening to the Sutra being explained. The more intelligent of you remember more. Those of average intelligence

remember less than the smart ones, and the duller ones remember even less. The rain of Dharma of the Thus Come One
falls in the same way. Those with greater wisdom get more
moisture. Those with average wisdom get average moisture.
Those with little wisdom get less moisture. Everyone is
listening to the same Sutra, but everyone understands the
doctrine on his or her level of understanding. It's different for everyone.

"But you are explaining so many things here--forests
and trees and grasses and clouds--I don't understand one
bit of this!"

If you know that you <u>don't</u> understand, that means that
you must understand <u>some</u> of it! If you really didn't understand, you wouldn't even know that you didn't understand.
If you know that you don't understand, you are on your way
to understanding. Why don't you understand it? Because
you've never heard it before. You haven't heard the Dharma
before, so it's quite natural that you don't understand it
the very first time you hear it. Still, if you know that
you don't understand "one bit," then that's the "one bit"
you <u>do</u> understand! Today you understand one tiny bit, tomorrow you'll understand two parts, and the next day, three
parts and so on. Day by day your understanding will grow.
Besides, I've lectured to you for so long, if you don't understand one bit, you are quite extraordinary in your own
way! Tomorrow you'll only understand half a bit and the
day after nothing at all.

"ONE WORTHY OF OFFERINGS, ONE OF PROPER AND UNIVER-
SAL KNOWLEDGE. To understand that the ten thousand dharmas are only the mind is called "proper knowledge." To
understand that mind gives rise to the ten thousand dharmas is called "universal knowledge." Proper and universal
knowledge is just understanding the mind. ONE WHOSE UN-
DERSTANDING AND CONDUCT ARE COMPLETE, Through cultivation
he attains the perfect fruition--Buddhahood. WELL-GONE ONE
WHO UNDERSTANDS THE WORLD. "Well gone" means that he has
gone to a good place. UNSURPASSED LORD. There is no one
higher than him. TAMING AND REGULATING HERO. He tames,
guides, and controls living beings. TEACHER OF GODS AND
HUMANS, THE BUDDHA, THE WORLD HONORED ONE." The Buddha
dares to say these things of himself. "THOSE WHO HAVE
NOT YET BEEN CROSSED OVER, I CROSS OVER. That is, those
who have not yet understood the Buddhadharma, I lead to
an understanding of it. I take them from the place where
there is right and wrong to the place beyond right and
wrong. I take them from the place where there is good and
evil to the place beyond good and evil. I take them from
the place where there is birth and death to the place
where there is no birth and death. I take them across.

'THOSE WHO HAVE NOT BEEN LIBERATED, I LIBERATE. I set
them free. I bring them to understanding. THOSE WHO HAVE
NOT YET BEEN PUT TO REST, I PUT TO REST." He makes those
living beings happy who have never known happiness. "THOSE
WHO HAVE NOT YET ATTAINED NIRVANA, I CAUSE TO ATTAIN NIR-

VANA. Those who haven't attained the fruition of Nirvana,
with its four virtues: permanence, happiness, true self,
and purity, I cause them to attain it, to attain the bliss
of still extinction.

"I KNOW THINGS AS THEY REALLY ARE, BOTH IN THE PRESENT
AND IN THE FUTURE. I AM THE ALL-KNOWING ONE." The Buddha
says this, and in his case it's true. He wasn't like the
person who once claimed to know everything. I asked him,
"If you know everything, then how many grains of rice did
you eat at lunch today?"

"I don't know!" he answered.

If you asked the Buddha, he would know.

'THE ALL-SEEING ONE, THE ONE WHO KNOWS THE WAY." He
knows the Way to cultivate. "THE ONE WHO OPENS THE WAY.
A pioneer among cultivators. THE ONE WHO PROCLAIMS THE
WAY. THE ENTIRE ASSEMBLY OF GODS, HUMANS, AND ASURAS
SHOULD COME HERE AND LISTEN TO THE DHARMA." Listen to
the lectures on the Dharma! So, as you sit here in this
lecture hall, you may not see a lot of people. But there
are very many gods, and dragons, and others of the eight-
fold division present. If you opened your Five Eyes and
had the Six Spiritual Penetrations you'd know: "The Lecture Hall is packed! It's standing room only! I can't
even find a place to stand, for heaven's sake!" It's prob-
ably better you can't see. If you could, you wouldn't
even have room to walk around.

Sutra: T 19b15

Then, countless thousands of myriads of millions of kinds of living beings came before the Buddha to hear the Dharma.

Outline:

> M2. Correlating that
> which is produced with
> that which produces.

Commentary:

THEN, COUNTLESS THOUSANDS OF MYRIADS OF MILLIONS OF KINDS... There are many different kinds OF LIVING BEINGS... They all CAME BEFORE THE BUDDHA to the Dharma Flower Assembly in order to hear The Dharma Flower Sutra.

Sutra: T 19b16

Then, the Thus Come One, contemplating the sharpness and dullness of the faculties of these living beings, their vigor or laxness, according to their capacity, spoke the Dharma for their sakes . . .

Outline:

> M3. Further correlating
> that which moistens to

that which is moistened.

N1. That which mois-

tens.

Commentary:

THEN, THE THUS COME ONE, CONTEMPLATING in detail THE

SHARPNESS AND DULLNESS OF THE FACULTIES OF THESE LIVING

BEINGS. "Faculties" also means "roots." There are many

different living beings. Some have sharp faculties, while

others have dull faculties. Some are smart, and some are

stupid. THEIR VIGOR OR LAXNESS. Vigorous ones go forward

and make progress. Lax ones are lazy. ACCORDING TO THEIR

CAPACITY HE SPOKE DHARMA FOR THEIR SAKES. To the vigorous

ones he spoke of vigor. To the lax ones he spoke of lax-

ness to cure them of their laziness and encourage them to

work harder. He spoke to each one just that dharma which

they would be able to receive according to their indivi-

dual capacities. If they weren't able to accept it, then

the Buddha wouldn't speak it. That is why, at first, the

Buddha did not teach the Real Dharma. He taught the Pro-

visional Dharma instead.

Sutra: T 19b 18
... in limitless varieties, causing them all
to rejoice and quickly attain good benefit.
After having heard this Dharma, all of these
living beings presently are at ease; in the

future, they will be born in a good place. By means of the Way, they will enjoy happiness and also be able to hear the Dharma. Having heard the Dharma, they will separate from all coverings and obstructions. Within all the dharmas, according to their powers, they will gradually gain entry to the Way.

Outline:

N2. That which is

moistened.

Commentary:

...IN LIMITLESS VARIETIES, the Buddha speaks all manner of dharmas, CAUSING THEM ALL TO REJOICE--to be happy. The Buddha spoke the Dharma to make living beings happy. He spoke whatever Dharma they would respond to happily. Once they were happy and interested, he gradually sent them down the Path to Buddhahood. AND QUICKLY ATTAIN GOOD BENEFIT. AFTER HAVING HEARD THIS DHARMA, ALL OF THESE LIVING BEINGS PRESENTLY ARE AT EASE; IN THE FUTURE, THEY WILL BE BORN IN A GOOD PLACE. In the present they are tranquil and at ease. In the future they may be born in the heavens or among wealthy humans.

BY MEANS OF THE WAY, THEY WILL ENJOY HAPPINESS. By cultivating the Way, they will become very happy. AND

ALSO BE ABLE TO HEAR THE DHARMA. HAVING HEARD THE DHARMA,
THEY WILL SEPARATE FROM ALL COVERINGS AND OBSTRUCTIONS.
If you wish to separate from obstacles, you must hear the
Dharma. If you don't hear the Dharma, you won't be able
to understand true principle, and you won't be able to
leave your obstructions. WITHIN ALL THE DHARMAS, ACCORD-
ING TO THEIR POWERS, THEY WILL GRADUALLY GAIN ENTRY TO THE
WAY. It happens very naturally, according to their abili-
ties. They gradually enter the Path of cultivation, gradually gain enlightenment, gradually become Buddhas, and
gradually end birth and death.

Sutra: T 19 b 21
   Just as that great cloud rains down on all
the grasses, trees, forests, and medicinal herbs
and each, according to its nature, fully receives
the moisture and grows...

Outline:

L2. Bringing up the
analogy again.

Commentary:
   JUST AS THAT GREAT CLOUD RAINS DOWN ON ALL THE GRASSES,
TREES, FORESTS, AND MEDICINAL HERBS. The various types of
vegetation represent the various kinds living beings. There
are Bodhisattvas, Sound Hearers, Pratyeka Buddhas, gods,

people, hell-beings, hungry ghosts, and animals. AND EACH, ACCORDING TO ITS NATURE, according to capacity... Each living being accepts that dharma which they can accept, and each grows accordingly. FULLY RECEIVES THE MOISTURE AND GROWS. The larger ones get more; the smaller ones get less. Those who are wise get more wisdom; those with less wisdom, get less. But, whether they get more or less, they all get some, and they all grow.

Sutra: T 19 b 23
...So, too, the Thus Come One speaks of a Dharma having one mark and one taste, that is to say: the mark of liberation, the mark of extinction, culminating in the wisdom of all modes.

Outline:

> K2. Corr. the different and yet not different.
>> L1. Corr. Proper.
>>> M1. Corr. "Grown from same ground and moistened by same rain."

Commentary:

...SO, TOO, IS THE DHARMA SPOKEN BY THE THUS COME
ONE OF ONE MARK. What is the one mark? It is the mark
of True Suchness of the essential nature of the minds of
living beings. The mark of True Suchness is like a piece
of ground, AND ONE TASTE. The one flavor is the Buddhadharma of the One Vehicle.

THAT IS TO SAY: THE MARK OF LIBERATION. Those living beings who haven't planted good roots are led to plant
them. Those who have planted them, nurture them so they
can grow. Those who have well-grown good roots find them
brought to maturity. And those whose good roots have ma-
tured are led to liberation.

THE MARK OF SEPARATION refers to leaving suffering
and distress. THE MARK OF EXTINCTION, the wiping out of
all affliction, CULMINATING IN THE WISDOM OF ALL MODES,
the wisdom of the Buddha. The Buddha speaks Dharma with
the hope that all living beings will one day attain the
Buddha-wisdom.

Sutra:T 19 b 25

*Those living beings who, hearing the Thus
Come One's Dharma, uphold read, recite and
cultivate it as taught will not themselves
be aware of the merit and virtue they obtain.*

Outline:

> M2. Corr. the dif-
> ferent grasses and
> trees.
>
>> N1. Corr. living
>> beings as like
>> grass and trees,
>> therefore, "un-
>> aware."

Commentary:

THOSE LIVING BEINGS WHO, HEARING THE THUS COME ONE'S DHARMA, UPHOLD, READ, RECITE, AND CULTIVATE IT AS TAUGHT, cultivating as the Buddha told them to and practicing what they have been told to practice in accord with Dharma. They WILL NOT THEMSELVES BE AWARE OF THE MERIT AND VIRTUE THEY OBTAIN. Things are pretty much the same here. You come to listen to the Buddhadharma. You have all changed a great deal for the better, although you yourselves may not be a-ware of this. "How have I changed?" you wonder. You are unaware of the fact that you've lost your bad habits now, and even if you wanted them back, you wouldn't know where to start looking for them!

Sutra: T 19 b 26

What is the reason? Only the Thus Come One knows the kinds, the marks, the substances, and

*the natures of these living beings, what they
are recollecting, what they are thinking, and
what they are cultivating; how they are recollecting, how they are thinking, and how
they are cultivating ; by means of what
dharma they recollect, by means of what
dharma they think, and by means of what
dharma they cultivate; and by means of
what dharma they obtain what dharma.
Living beings dwell on a variety of levels.
Only the Thus Come One sees them as they
really are, clearly and without obstruction.*

Outline:

> N2. Showing that
> only the Thus Come
> One knows the be-
> ings. He is, there-
> fore, like the
> great cloud.

Commentary:

WHAT IS THE REASON? ONLY THE THUS COME ONE KNOWS
THE KINDS: There are various kinds of living beings.
There are Buddhas, Bodhisattvas, Sound Hearers, Condi-

tioned-Enlightened Ones, gods, people, asuras, ghosts, hell-beings, and animals--all those in the ten Dharma Realms. Depending on one's karma, one becomes one of them. THE MARKS. This refers to their external appearances. THE SUBSTANCES, that is, their basic make-up, AND THE NATURES, their inward disposition.

So, those are the Four Dharmas: kind, mark, substance, and nature.

WHAT THEY ARE RECOLLECTING, WHAT THEY ARE THINKING, AND WHAT THEY ARE CULTIVATING: There are also Three Dharmas: Hearing, thinking, and cultivating. Hearing refers to hearing the Dharma by listening to lectures on the Sutra. Through our hearing we gain the wisdom of hearing. After you have listened to the Dharma for a while, without realizing it yourself you will grow wiser. For example, some of my disciples can explain the Ten Dwellings and the Ten Grounds. If they hadn't listened to the Buddhadharma, they would not be able to do this. When you study the Buddhadharma, you gain wisdom. This is called the wisdom of hearing.

Thinking refers to meditation, that is, practicing the Four Dhyanas and stilling one's thought processes. This is wisdom of thinking. One thinks about the principles one has heard and chooses the right path to follow.

Once you have thought it through carefully, then you start cultivating. You must work hard and never, ever be lazy. You must cultivate in the morning, in the evening,

and all day long. Then you will gain the wisdom of cultivation. You must approach your cultivation with wisdom.
If you lack wisdom and cultivate blindly, you may get off
the track and end up cultivating yourself right into hell.
HOW THEY ARE RECOLLECTING, HOW THEY ARE THINKING, AND
WHAT THEY ARE CULTIVATING. They recollect the Buddha, the
they think about the Dharma, they cultivate the deeds of
the Sangha. They constantly in every thought recollect,
think about, and cultivate the principle of the Buddhadharma. Clearly, calmly, and without false thinking, they
think about the doctrines and then cultivate them. BY
MEANS OF WHAT DHARMA THEY RECOLLECT, BY MEANS OF WHAT DHAR-
MA THEY THINK, AND BY MEANS OF WHAT DHARMA THEY CULTIVATE.
They recollect, think, and cultivate in accord with Proper
Dharma. They cultivate according to the laws of cause and
effect. They know that whatever cause they plant, it will
bear a corresponding fruit.

AND BY MEANS OF WHAT DHARMA, THEY OBTAIN WHAT DHARMA.
You use Buddhadharma, you get Buddhahood. You use demonic
dharma, you get demonic dharma. There are also Two Dharmas: Cause and effect. "By means of what dharma" is the
cause and "they obtain what dharma" is the effect. As is
the cause, so is the effect. According to the causes planted by the Five Vehicles, they obtain corresponding effects.

LIVING BEINGS DWELL ON A VARIETY OF LEVELS: This is
the One Dharma. It refers to the Seven Expedients dwelling
in the Seven Positions. The Seven Expedients are: the Ve-

hicle of Gods, the Vehicle of Humans, the Vehicle of Sound
Hearers, the Vehicle of Conditioned Enlightened Ones, the
Vehicle of the Storehouse Teaching Bodhisattvas, the Vehicle of the Penetrating Teaching Bodhisattvas, and the Vehicle of the Special Teaching Bodhisattvas.

ONLY THE THUS COME ONE SEES THEM AS THEY REALLY ARE.
Living beings themselves are not aware of their various
states. Only the Thus Come One really sees them. CLEARLY
AND WITHOUT OBSTRUCTION. He knows them from beginning to
end, inside and out, thoroughly, completely, to their very
depths. Ordinary people might understand the beginning
but not understand the end, or else they won't understand
the beginning but will understand the end. They can't understand both at once. You might know how beings are born
and not know about how they die, or vice-vers.

He understands the inside and the outside, clearly
without any obstruction. As long as one clearly understands, then there is no obstacle. If one doesn't clearly
understand, then there are obstacles. Therefore, only
the Buddha can really understand and be without obstacles.

There is a verse about obstacles, which runs:

> I vow to eradicate the three obstructions
> and all affliction.
> I vow to attain wisdom that is truly bright.
> I vow that all disasters quickly melt away.
> And in every life I vow to practice the
> Bodhisattva Path.

There are three obstructions: The obstruction of karma, the obstruction of retribution, and the obstruction of afflictions. One should vow to attain wisdom. With wisdom you can have clear understanding; otherwise, you cannot. One should vow to get rid of all disasters and calamities and always practice the Bodhisattva Path, benefitting oneself and benefitting others.

Sutra: T 19c2

... Just as those grasses, trees, and forests and all the medicinal herbs do not know themselves whether their natures are superior, middle, or inferior.

Outline:

> N3. Living beings unaware of their own natures.

Commentary:

The Buddha knows clearly and without obstruction, but the living beings who are moistened by the Dharma are not aware themselves of their own capacities, and THOSE GRASSES, TREES, AND FORESTS AND ALL THE MEDICINAL HERBS DO NOT KNOW THEMSELVES WHETHER THEIR NATURES ARE SUPERIOR, MIDDLE, OR INFERIOR.

Sutra: T 19 c 3

The Thus Come One knows the Dharma
of one mark, of one flavor, that is to say: the
mark of liberation, the mark of separation,
the mark of extinction, the mark of ultimate Nirvana which is constantly still and
extinct and which in the end returns to
emptiness.

Outline:

> L2. Conclusion
>
> M1. Conclusion "differ-
> ent is just not differ-
> ent."

Commentary:

THE THUS COME ONE KNOWS THE DHARMA OF ONE MARK, the
mark of True Suchness of the mind and nature of living beings. OF ONE FLAVOR refers to the cultivation of the One
Vehicle and certification to the wonderful principle. THAT
IS TO SAY: THE MARK OF LIBERATION, THE MARK OF SEPARATION,
THE MARK OF EXTINCTION. Now, originally there is no mark
of liberation, no mark of separation, no mark of extinction. These marks are spoken of to counteract the attach-
ments of living beings. Think it over: If it is really
liberation, how could it retain a mark? If it is really

separation, how could there still be a mark. If it's really separation, then it should be separate from even the concept of separation. So why do we bring up the "mark of separation?" If we didn't, living beings wouldn't have anything to relate to, and it would be difficult for them to believe. THE MARK OF EXTINCTION is also without a mark. In general, all dharmas have been been swept away, and all marks have been left behind. Not a single dharma is postulated. THE MARK OF ULTIMATE NIRVANA WHICH IS CONSTANTLY STILL AND EXTINCT. The Dharma of one mark and one flavor ultimately returns to Nirvana with its four virtues of permanence, bliss, true self, and purity. The mark of ultimate Nirvana, constantly still and extinct, is also not a mark. If it had a mark, it would not be still and extinct.

WHICH IN THE END RETURNS TO EMPTINESS, wherein there is not even the mark of emptiness.

Sutra: T 19c5

Already understanding this the Buddha contemplates the desires in the minds of living beings and protects them. For this reason he does not immediately speak of the wisdom of all modes.

Outline:

M2. Explaining why he doesn't immediately

> speak the wisdom of
> all modes.

Commentary:

UNDERSTANDING THIS, THE BUDDHA, having, while in the midst of marks, transcended marks, then CONTEMPLATES THE DESIRES IN THE MINDS OF LIVING BEINGS. Basically, there is no dharma to be spoken, and there are no marks to be obtained. However, living beings all have their fondnesses. If you started right out teaching them that there was nothing at all--not a single dharma--and that all dharmas are empty, living beings wouldn't believe it. Not only would they not believe it, they would slander it as well. "If dharmas are basically empty, why are you speaking about them, anyway?" they would ask. So the Buddha took a long look at living beings' minds. He knew that they were not ready to accept the true dharma. Living beings have many faults which they must gradually be encouraged to stop. If you try to do it all at once by telling them it's all empty, they won't be able to do it.

AND PROTECTS THEM... By refraining from speaking the Real Dharma and speaking the Provisional instead, he protects living beings from slandering the Dharma.

FOR THIS REASON HE DOES NOT IMMEDIATELY SPEAK OF THE WISDOM OF ALL MODES. That is the reason why the Buddha does not immediately speak the Dharma of the Real Mark. He waits a bit. The wisdom of all modes is the real mark

Prajna. The Buddha takes a look at the causes, conditions, and dispositions of living beings. Upon seeing that they haven't ripened yet, he refrains from speaking to them of the wisdom of all modes and the real mark Prajna.

Sutra: T 19 c 6

Kashyapa, you are all very rare in your ability to know that the Thus Come One speaks the Dharma as it is appropriate, and in your ability to believe and accept it. Why is this? All the Buddhas, the World Honored Ones speak an appropriate Dharma which is difficult to understand, difficult to know.

Outline:

I2. Concluding praise and narration.

Commentary:

"KASHYAPA, YOU ARE ALL, all of you Sound Hearers, VERY RARE, rare indeed, IN YOUR ABILITY TO KNOW THAT THE THUS COME ONE SPEAKS THE DHARMA AS IT IS APPROPRIATE, you are rare because you understand that the Buddha speaks the Dharma in accord with the inclinations of the beings he teaches, in accord with their dispositions, and in accord with their causes and conditions. AND IN YOUR ABILITY TO BELIEVE AND ACCEPT IT. WHY IS THIS? ALL THE BUDDHAS, THE

1066

WORLD HONORED ONES, SPEAK AN APPROPRIATE DHARMA WHICH IS DIFFICULT TO UNDERSTAND, DIFFICULT TO KNOW. The Dharma spoken by the Buddhas is supreme, profound, and wonderful. So it is not easy to understand.

Sutra: T 19c8

At that time the World Honored One, wishing to restate this meaning spoke verses, saying:

Destroyer of existence, the Dharma King
Manifests within the world;
According to living beings' desires,
He teaches the Dharma in various ways.
The Thus Come One, out of veneration
For this wisdom, deep and far-reaching,
Has long remained silent on this import-
   ant matter,
Being in no hurry to set it forth.
Those with wisdom, if they heard it,
Would be able to believe and understand it,
But those lacking wisdom would doubt it
And thereby lose it for a long time
For this reason, Kashyapa,
It is spoken in accord with their powers

Employing various conditions
To lead them to the right view.

Outline:

H2. Verse

I1. Verses of Dharma.

Commentary:

AT THAT TIME, THE WORLD HONORED ONE, Shakyamuni Buddha, compassionately wishing to teach living beings, and WISHING TO RESTATE THIS MEANING, SPOKE VERSES, SAYING:

DESTROYER OF EXISTENCE, THE DHARMA KING/ "Existence" refers to the presence of cause and effect. How does the Buddha break through cause and effect? On the part of living beings, the laws of cause and effect always apply. If you plant a good cause, you reap a good fruit; if you plant an evil cause, you reap an evil fruit. But, the Buddha, having reached enlightenment through his cultivation, is no longer bound by cause and effect. He has broken through existence, through the "unstoppable" process of cause and effect. The Dharma King is the Buddha, the King who speaks the Dharma. Those who leave home should learn to speak the Dharma like the Buddha, with his Four Kinds of Unobstructed Eloquence and his Eight Sounds. In speaking the Dharma, we represent the Buddha, the Dharma King.

MANIFESTS WITHIN THE WORLD/ The Buddha manifests with-

in the world to smash through all of existence. He can't
do it all at once, however. ACCORDING TO LIVING BEINGS'
DESIRES/ HE TEACHES THE DHARMA IN VARIOUS WAYS/ He fig-
ures out what living beings like and, going along with
them, teaches them bit by bit. He doesn't speak the Dharma in just one way. There are many ways to speak it.
There are Five Periods and Eight Teachings.

THE THUS COME ONE, OUT OF VENERATION/ FOR THIS WISDOM,
DEEP AND FAR-REACHING/ Because the real mark Prajna wisdom
is to be revered greatly, being profound and far-reaching.
HAS LONG REMAINED SILENT ON THIS IMPORTANT MATTER/ Because it is so deep and so lofty, those of ordinary, shal-
low understanding cannot penetrate it. Because it is so
vast in scope, it isn't appropriate for those of the Small
Vehicle. Therefore, the Buddha has sized them up as Small
Vehicle types, and he cannot speak the Great Vehicle Dharma to them. He has kept silent on the matter for a long
time. "Long" refers to the time from the end of the Ava-
tamsaka Period up to the beginning of the Lotus Flower-
Nirvana Period--over thirty years. During those thirty
years, he did not set forth the real teaching; he spoke the
provisional teaching instead. He did not speak the real
mark Prajna, that is, the docrtine of the One Buddha Vehicle. It's been a long, long time since he spoke the important matter. He kept it to himself. Why? If he had
spoken of the real wisdom, the real teaching, living beings would not only not believe, they would even slander

it. BEING IN NO HURRY TO SET IT FORTH/ The Buddha certainly

has a lot of patience.

THOSE WITH WISDOM, IF THEY HEARD IT/ WOULD BE ABLE TO

BELIEVE AND UNDERSTAND IT/ They would believe and accept

the doctrine of the Great Vehicle Buddhadharma. But, THOSE

LACKING WISDOM WOULD DOUBT IT/ THEREBY LOSING IT FOR A LONG

TIME/ If you spoke to them in terms of the Great Vehicle

saying--"originally, there was no bondage, and now there

is no need to seek liberation. Originally, there was no

uniting with marks, and so now there is no need to separate

from marks. Originally there was no mark of production and

now there is no need to speak of a mark of extinction"--

if you tried to teach them something that truthful and out-

in-front, then they would not believe it. They would have

many doubts. That's why you have to apply clever expedient

devices and use all kinds of analogies to bring them to un-

derstanding.

Stupid people would not belive. They would think,

"Hmmm...this all sounds too nihilistic to me. What does he

mean, 'There's nothing at all?' If there's nothing at all,

we're finished! We've had it! If it all reverts to empti-

ness, what are we doing studying this? There's nothing

to study!" Having given rise to doubt, they cut off the

seeds of the Great Vehicle, which is equivalent to cutting

off the seeds of Buddhahood, and cutting off the seeds

of being living beings, and they thereby lose it for a

long time.

FOR THIS REASON, KASHYAPA/ IT IS SPOKEN IN ACCORD
WITH THEIR POWERS/ EMPLOYING VARIOUS CONDITIONS/ Expedient, clever provisional dharmas and analogies TO LEAD
THEM TO THE RIGHT VIEW/ To bring them to right knowledge
and the right views.

Sutra: T 19c15

Kashyapa, you should know
It is like a great cloud
Rising above the world
And covering all
A wisdom cloud filled with moisture
Illuminated with lightening flashes
And vibrating with thunderous roars
It brings delight to all,
Obscuring the light of the sun,
Refreshing the earth
The cloud lowers and expands
As if one could reach out and touch it.
It rains equally everywhere
Falling alike in the four directions
Pouring without measure
Saturating all the land.

Outline:

    I2. Verses of setting up
    parable.

        J1. Verses of not dif-
        ferent and yet different.

            K1. Verses of that
            which moistens as
            not different.

Commentary:

KASHYAPA, YOU SHOULD KNOW/ the Thus Come One speaks the Dharma. IT IS LIKE A GREAT CLOUD/ RISING ABOVE THE WORLD/ and covering the three thousand, great thousand worlds, A WISDOM CLOUD FILLED WITH MOISTURE/ The cloud represents the Buddha's real wisdom, whose rain moistens the hearts of all living beings. ILLUMINATED WITH LIGHT- NING FLASHES/ The Buddha emits limitless light, like the flashes of lightning. AND VIBRATING WITH THUNDROUS ROARS/ The thunder represents the sound of the Buddha's voice speaking the Dharma. IT BRINGS DELIGHT TO ALL/ Causing all living beings to feel happiness in their hearts. OB- SCURING THE LIGHT OF THE SUN/ The light of the Buddha's wisdom outshines the light of all outsides ways; it out- shines the light of the ninety-five deviant lights. With- out the light of the Buddha's wisdom, non-Buddhists would appear to have principle. But, once their teachings are compared to the Buddhadharma, their deviant wisdom is revealed for what it is and is outshone by the Buddha's wisdom. REFRESHING THE EARTH/ This is also an analogy. It represents the Buddha using the clear, pure refreshing wiswisdom to cool off the earth's ninety-eight kinds of affliction. THE CLOUD LOWERS AND EXPANDS/ AS IF ONE COULD REACH OUT AND TOUCH IT/ IT RAINS EQUALLY EVERYWHERE/ The wisdom of the Buddha's words of Dharma universally moisten all living beings. FALLING ALIKE IN THE FOUR DIRECTIONS/ This represents the Eight Sounds and Four Types of Eloquence of the Buddha. POURING WITHOUT MEASURE/ SATURATING ALL THE LAND/ In the Four Books, there is the saying:

Everything under heaven
is the land of the King;

Everywhere all the land receives moisture, just as all living beings receive the moisture of the Buddhadharma.

In these verses Shakyamuni Buddha praises Mahakashyapa and all the Sound Hearer disciples as being extremely rare, because they like to hear the Dharma the Buddha speaks. Because they like to study the Buddhadharma, the Buddha says that they are "rare." What is meant by "rare?" It means that there are few such people. In this world, there are many people, but very few of them get to listen to the Dharma; this makes them rare. If you put on a play or show a film, a lot of people will come to watch. If you have a gambling house, a lot of people will come. But here we lecture on the Sutras all the time, and still only these few people come to listen. Sometimes they come and sometimes they don't! Such people are rare indeed. So, take a look at yourselves, and you will know that you are rare people. There are few like you. Some of you go to school, and some of you have jobs and go to work--you do various things. Some of you take care of your homes, and some of you work outside, and yet in the evenings you all find time to come and listen to lectures on the Sutras. Very rare!

Sutra: T 19c 20

> In the mountains, streams and steep valleys,
> In deep recesses, there grow
> Grasses, trees, and herbs,
> And trees, both great and small,
> The grains, shoots, and plants,
> The sugar-cane and the grape vine;
> All are nourished by the rain,
> And none fail to be enriched.
> The parched ground is soaked,
> The herbs and trees together flourish.
> Issuing from that cloud
> Water of a single flavor
> Moistens grasses, trees and forests

Each according to its measure
All of the trees,
Great, medium and small,
According to their size
Can grow and develop.
When reached by that single rain
The roots, stalks, branches, and leaves,
Flowers and fruits with luster and color,
All are fresh and shining.

Outline:

> K2. Verses about receiving
> different levels of moisture.

Commentary:

IN THE MOUNTAINS, STREAMS, AND DEEP VALLEYS/ The mountains represent the Great Bodhisattvas. The streams represent all the great Disciples. IN DEEP RECESSES, THERE GROW/ GRASSES, TREES, AND HERBS/ The analogy gives the three kinds of grass and two kinds of trees. The three kinds of grass are: the Vehicle of People, the Vehicle of Gods, and the Vehicles of the Sound Hearers and Condition-enlightened Ones. The two kinds of trees are the Bodhisattvas. AND TREES, BOTH GREAT AND SMALL/

THE GRAINS, SHOOTS, AND PLANTS/ The text says literally, "The hundred grains." The word "hundred" represents the ten good deeds, each of which is multiplied by ten, making a hundred good deeds. The shoots and plants are all the living beings. THE SUGAR-CANE AND THE GRAPE VINE/ Sugar cane grows in stalks which represents both Dhyana samadhi and the spiritual powers derived from it. Grapes grow in clusters, representing the use of one single wisdom door to cut off many, many doubts. ALL ARE NOURISHED BY THE RAIN/ AND NONE FAIL TO BE ENRICHED/ They all grow. They each receive the share of rain that they should receive. THE PARCHED GROUND IS SOAKED/ "Parched ground" refers to living beings who have not planted good roots, who have not heard the Buddhadharma. These living beings are also nourished by the Dharma-rain and gain advantage. THE HERBS AND TREES TOGETHER FLOURISH/ They grow and flourish. ISSUING FROM THAT CLOUD/ WATER OF A SINGLE FLAVOR/ The One Vehicle Buddhadharma MOISTENS GRASSES, TREES, AND FORESTS/ all living beings EACH ACCORDING TO ITS MEASURE/ They receive the benefit they deserve. ALL OF THE TREES/ GREAT, MEDIUM, AND SMALL/ ACCORDING TO THEIR SIZE/ CAN GROW AND DEVELOP/ WHEN REACHED BY THAT SINGLE RAIN/ THE ROOTS, STALKS, BRANCHES, AND LEAVES/ FLOWERS, AND FRUITS WITH LUSTER AND COLOR/ ALL ARE FRESH AND SHINING/ They are fresh, sparkling, and beautiful.

Sutra: T 19c 28

According to their substance and marks,
And natures, either great or small

They alike receive moisture
And each one flourishes.

Outline:

> J2. Verses of "different and
> yet not different."

Commentary:

ACCORDING TO THEIR SUBSTANCE, MARKS/ The large ones
get much moisture, the middle-sized ones get less, and the
smaller ones get even less. Each gets what it deserves.
AND NATURES, EITHER GREAT OR SMALL/ THEY ALIKE RECEIVE
MOISTURE/ AND EACH ONE FLOURISHES/ For example, we are now
giving lectures on the Sutra. The lecturing could be con-
sidered one, big rain-cloud. Of those who come to listen,
some will understand one thing and some will understand
many, many principles. Some will, as the saying goes, hear
one thing and understand one thing, while others will hear
one thing and understand ten, or even a hundred! Some people will change some of their small, bad habits and gain
small benefit. Some will change their major, bad habits
and thereby obtain great benefit. Some will get rid of all
their bad habits completely, gaining the greatest benefit.

When you have heard and understood the Dharma, it
is like having been moistened by the rain. When you get
rid of your bad habits, your wisdom-life and Dharma-body
flourish and grow, your wisdom develops and sheds its

light. Before, when you had all those bad habits, you
didn't realize that your body gave off no light at all.
Now, for every bit of habit energy that you get rid of,
you emit that much more light.

Sutra: T 19c 28

The Buddha, in the same way
Manifests within the world
Just like a great cloud
Covering over everything.
Having come into the world
For the sake of living beings,
He discriminates and expounds
The reality of all dharmas.
The Great Sage, the World Honored One,
In the midst of the multitudes
Of gods and humans
Proclaims these words saying:
"I am the Thus Come One
The doubly complete honored one.
I appear within the world
Like a great cloud
Moistening all
The dried-out living beings,
So they all leave suffering

And gain peace and bliss
Worldly joy
And the joy of Nirvana.
All gods and humans assembled here
Listen singlemindedly and well.
You should all come here
To behold the Unsurpassed Honored One,
I am the World Honored One,
The one beyond compare.
To bring peace and ease to living beings
I manifest within the world
And for the sake of the assembly speak
The sweet dew of pure Dharma
The Dharma of a single flavor,
That of liberation and Nirvana.
Using a single, wondrous sound
I proclaim this principle
Constantly creating the causes and con-
    ditions
For the Great Vehicle.

Outline:

Commentary:

THE BUDDHA, IN THE SAME WAY/ MANIFESTS WITHIN THE
WORLD/ JUST LIKE A GREAT CLOUD/ COVERING OVER EVERYTHING/
The Buddha covers all living beings with the rain of Dharma.
HAVING COME INTO THE WORLD/ FOR THE SAKE OF LIVING
BEINGS/ HE DISCRIMINATES AND EXPOUNDS/ THE REALITY OF ALL
DHARMAS/ When he sees people, he speaks human dharma; when
he meets gods, he speaks heavenly dharma; when he meets
those of the Two Vehicles, he speaks the dharma of the Two
Vehicles. When he encounters those of the Great Vehicle,
he expounds that teaching. "Discriminates" does not mean
that he uses his discriminating mind to speak the Dharma.
It means that he speaks Dharma in accord with living beings' potentials. For the sake of the real, he expounds
the provisional. All expedient Dharmas are spoken for the
sake of the real teaching.

THE GREAT SAGE, THE WORLD HONORED ONE/ The Buddha is
the great Sage. IN THE MIDST OF THE MULTITUDES/ OF GODS

AND HUMANS/ PROCLAIMS THESE WORDS, SAYING/ "I AM THE THUS COME ONE/ THE DOUBLY COMPLETE AND HONORED ONE/ "Doubly complete" means that he is complete with both blessings and wisdom. In the cause ground, he did many good deeds, so his blessings are complete. It's not enough just to have blessings and to have no wisdom. The Buddha is also complete in wisdom. As the saying goes:

> One who cultivates blessings and not wisdom,
> is like an elephant wearing a necklace;
> One who cultivates wisdom and no blessings,
> is like an Arhat with an empty bowl.

Those who cultivate blessings without cultivating wisdom do not listen to the Sutras; they merely practice good deeds. They may pile up many blessings, but they have no wisdom. This makes them like a big, dumb elephant. Elephants aren't really as stupid as they are awkward. They are so big with such big legs! They are too big to fly. In fact, they can't get off the ground. Now, picture an elephant wearing a necklace. The person who adorns himself with blessings is like that--useless.

If you only listen to the Sutras and Dharma and fail to do good deeds and help others, you are like an Arhat with an empty bowl. In the future when you become an Arhat, you will travel all over with an empty bowl; no one will make offerings to you. Why not? Because you never practiced good deeds. What do you think of that! Here you are, a certified Arhat and hungry all day long! You

go from day to day with an empty stomach. Why? Because
you only listened to Dharma and did not do good deeds.
The Buddha is doubly complete in wisdom and blessings.
I APPEAR WITHIN THE WORLD/ LIKE A GREAT CLOUD/ MOISTENING
ALL/ THE DRIED-OUT LIVING BEINGS/ living beings who have
not heard the Buddhadharma. Once living beings have heard
the Buddhadharma, they are no longer dried-out, they are
"moist." SO THEY ALL LEAVE SUFFERING/ and attain bliss--
AND GAIN PEACE AND BLISS/ WORLDLY JOY/ AND THE JOYS OF
NIRVANA/ both transcendental and worldly happiness. ALL
GODS AND HUMANS ASSEMBLED HERE/ LISTEN SINGLEMINDEDLY AND
WELL/ to the Buddhadharma. YOU SHOULD ALL COME HERE/ TO
BEHOLD THE UNSURPASSED HONORED ONE/ draw near to and rev-
erently worship the Buddha.

I AM THE WORLD HONORED ONE/ Honored both in and beyond the world. THE ONE BEYOND COMPARE/ No one is as
high as the Buddha.

In the heavens and below, there's no one
like the Buddha.
In the ten direction worlds, he is beyond
compare.
I've seen everything in the world there
is to see,
And in it nothing can compare to the Buddha.

TO BRING PEACE AND EASE TO LIVING BEINGS/ I MANIFEST WITH-
IN THE WORLD/ AND, FOR THE SAKE OF THE ASSEMBLY, SPEAK/
THE SWEET DEW OF PURE DHARMA/--the wonderful Dharma, which
is like sweet dew.

THE DHARMA OF A SINGLE FLAVOR/ THAT OF LIBERATION
AND NIRVANA/ USING A SINGLE, WONDROUS SOUND/ I PROCLAIM
THIS PRINCIPLE/ This is the Dharma of the One Buddha Ve-
hicle. The Buddha proclaims it in The Wonderful Dharma
Flower Sutra. CONSTANTLY, FOR MAKING THE CAUSAL CONDI-
TIONS/ OF THE GREAT VEHICLE/ The Buddha employs all man-
ner of causes and conditions to teach the Great Vehicle
Dharma.

Sutra: T 20a13
> I contemplate all
> Everywhere as equal,
> Without "this" or "that"
> And without thoughts of love or hate.
> I have no greed or attachment,
> And no limitations or obstacles.
> Constantly for everyone,
> I speak the Dharma, equally,
> Speaking for a single person,
> As I would for the multitudes.
> I constantly expound and proclaim the
>   Dharma

And have no other work:
Coming, going, sitting and standing
I never grow weary,
Filling the entire world,
Like the moisture of the universal rain.

Outline:

K2. Verses correlating that
which produces with that
which is produced.

Commentary:

I CONTEMPLATE ALL/ EVERYWHERE AS EQUAL/ This line
shows us the great compassion of the Buddha. The Buddha
never says, "I am the highest. I created all things, and
they are all mine." The Buddha says that he "teaches"
the ten thousand things. He instructs them to leave the
deviant and return to the proper, to cast aside confusion
and return to enlightenment. He doesn't say, "I alone
am enlightened. You are all confused."

He is not like the Lord who created all things who
says, "I created all of you." If you created all this,
why did you make such a mess of it? Why didn't you do a
better job? Why did you create evil? Why did you create
evil people who harm the good people? That's being even
worse than a common thief!

The Buddha does not claim to have created all things.

He rescues all things. Those who do not understand the Buddhadharma, he leads to understand it. Those who have not yet awakened, he leads to awakening. He doesn't say, "I made all of you." The Buddha saves all living beings, and having done so, there are no living beings whom he has saved. He saves all living beings but does not claim to have done so. That means that he is truly egalitarian.

I CONTEMPLATE ALL/ EVERYWHERE AS EQUAL/ WITHOUT "THIS" OR "THAT"/ AND WITHOUT THOUGHTS OF LOVE OR HATE/ Without discriminations between this and that, there is no love or hate. When one discriminates between this and that, then love and hate exist. "I love this person, and I hate that person. I love what pleases me and what does not please me, I hate." If you can not love the things that please you and not hate the things you dislike and not discriminate between this and that, then you are equal in your views without the concepts of this and that. You have knocked down that Mount Sumeru.

The text says, I HAVE NO GREED OR ATTACHMENT/ How can the Buddha say this? How can the Buddha be without greed or attachment? It's simply because he has no thought of love or hate. Don't you agree that if you have love and hate, you will also have greed and attachment? You will be greedy for things you desire and try to avoid things you dislike.

AND NO LIMITATIONS OR OBSTACLES/ If you love or hate something, those emotions form your limitations concerning them. That makes for an obstruction.

CONSTANTLY, FOR EVERYONE/ I SPEAK THE DHARMA, EQUAL-
LY/ SPEAKING FOR A SINGLE PERSON/ AS I WOULD FOR THE MUL-
TITUDES/ When you practice lecturing, don't think, "Not
as many people come to hear my lectures as they do to hear
his! Jees! They don't want to listen to me. This is
too humiliating. Really! They just don't want to hear
me!!" Here, you give rise to all kinds of love and hate
and so on... The Buddha always speaks the Dharma for
everyone. One person is many; many people are one person.
One is many; many is one. Speaking the Dharma equally
means that you do not notice whether there are many or
just a few in the audience. Neither many nor few; nothing
far and nothing near. I am speaking the Dharma here right
now, and they may even be listening to me in Hong Kong!
"Oh! Our Teacher is in America lecturing The Dharma Flower Sutra. Let's get some tapes and listen." So, I lecture for Hong Kong as I would for America, and I lecture
for America as I would for Hong Kong. That's called "not
discriminating between near and far," speaking Dharma
equally for those both near and far.

What are you laughing at? I am speaking true, real
principle. There's nothing in it to laugh at! And there's
nothing in it not to laugh at, either.

I CONSTANTLY EXPOUND AND PROCLAIM THE DHARMA/ Haven't
I told you before that as long as I have breath left, I
will speak the Dharma. If I quit speaking the Dharma, my

breath will also cease. So none of you can retire or retreat from speaking the Dharma. If you do, it's very in-
auspicious. AND HAVE NO OTHER WORK/ We who study the Buddhadharma, must speak the Buddhadharma. There are several
of you now who are headed to Taiwan to take the precepts,
so I am speaking the precept-taking Dharma to you. When
you have received the precepts, there may be as many as
fifty, or five hundred, or five thousand people in America
who will follow you to take precepts as well. People will
see that you are not even afraid of starving to death.
They don't ask for offerings either. They are really
practicing the Buddhadharma." Those who come after you
will want to imitate you in not fearing starving to death.
They will want to imitate your temperaments, because you
are happy all day long and never get angry. They will
want to keep the precepts pure as the two Bhikshunis who
don't eat after noon. That's really wonderful!

On the other hand, if you come back from taking precepts and sleep all day, eat fine food and wear fine
clothes, no one will believe in you, and the Buddhadharma
will become extinct. To say nothing of five, there won't
be even one cultivator in America! The responsibility for
the flowering of American Buddhism rests with the five of
you. I'm not trying to frighten you, but, in fact, you
are the pioneers of Western Buddhism. There have never
been so many people from the West to go to take the precepts of the Great Vehicle. This is a new page in history.

If they ask you who your teacher is, however, just
say, "Shakyamuni Buddha." Don't say it's anyone else.
Shakyamuni Buddha is your original teacher. If they ask
who you study under, say you study with the Pratimoskha,
the moral code. Say that you take the precepts as your
teacher. The Buddha, in truth, instructed his disciples
after his Nirvana to take the precepts as their teacher.
I don't want you to mention my name, because I have no
cultivation and no Way virtue. I am not fit to be anyone's teacher. Also, I don't want to be anyone's teacher.
There are a lot of fine gods in the heavens, but I don't
want to go there. How much the less do I want to hang
out in the human realm!

AND HAVE NO OTHER WORK/ I just speak the Dharma.
COMING, GOING, SITTING, AND STANDING/ This means walking,
standing, sitting, reclining. FILLING THE ENTIRE WORLD/
LIKE THE MOISTURE OF THE UNIVERSAL RAIN/ Standing, walking, sitting, and reclining, I am at all times speaking
the Dharma. I am never lazy. I speak the Dharma while
I am standing. I speak the Dharma while I am sitting.
I even speak the Dharma while I am sleeping! How do I
do that? In my dreams I teach and transform all the
dreaming living beings.

Why does the Buddha speak the Dharma? Because living beings are too dried out. If they didn't receive the
moisture of the Buddhadharma, they would wither up and
die. Once they are dead, if you speak Dharma to them it

won't bring them back to life. So, he gives them the Dharma rain to refresh them and help them grow. The rain moistens all the three grasses and two kinds of trees-- all the vegetation.

Sutra: T20a18

For the noble, the lowly, the superior and in-
ferior,
Those who keep precepts
And those who break them,
Those with perfect awesome manner
And those not perfect,
Those with right views and those with
deviant views
The sharp rooted, the dull rooted
I send down equally the Dharma rain
And never grow weary.

Outline:

K3. Verses further correlating that which moistens with that which is moistened.

L1. Correlating that which moistens.

Commentary:

FOR THE NOBLE, LOWLY, SUPERIOR, AND INFERIOR/ For
those of noble birth, for the lower classes, for the officials, and the common folk, THOSE WHO KEEP PRECEPTS
AND THOSE WHO BREAK THEM/ Perhaps there are left-home people who sternly maintain the moral code, or perhaps they
break those precepts. THOSE WITH PERFECT AWESOME MANNER/
AND THOSE NOT PERFECT/ Keeping precepts is maintaining
Vinaya. Breaking the precepts means violating that code.
There are three thousand aspects to the awesome manner.
There is a proper way to walk, to sit, to stand, and to
recline. In all four comportments, there is a proper,
awesome deportment. Some have not perfected it. They do
not stand, sit, walk or recline properly. THOSE WITH
RIGHT VIEWS AND THOSE WITH DEVIANT VIEWS/ Right views
means that, when improper matters are being discussed,
you do not listen.

> If it's not proper, don't look at it.
> If it's not proper, don't listen to it.
> If it's not proper, don't speak about it.
> If it's not proper, don't do it.

That's right views. If you look and listen, speak and do
things which are not in accord with principle, that means
you have deviant views.

THE SHARP ROOTED, THE DULL ROOTED/ Sharp means intel-

ligent. They hear the Dharma and gain enlightenment.
Dull means stupid. Stupid people may listen to Sturas for
a long time and still have no idea what the Buddhadharma
is. They won't cultivate giving, morality, patience, vig-
or, samadhi, or wisdom. Dull-rooted people can't accept
the Buddhadharma.

However, all these different types of living beings
are not discriminated by the Buddha, who says, I SEND DOWN
EQUALLY THE DHARMA RAIN/ Equally, he rains the Dharma rain
on all living beings. The Buddha is like a great rain
cloud filled with Dharma rain which all living beings receive.

AND NEVER GROW WEARY/ The Buddha is never lazy in
speaking the Dharma to living beings. He never gets
tired. To propagate the Buddhadharma, he forgets his
body, mind, nature, and life. The Buddha never gets
tired of teaching the Dharma.

Sutra: T 20 a 21

All living beings
Who hear my Dharma
Receive it according to their power
And dwell on various levels.
They may dwell among humans or gods,
Or Wheel Turning Sage Kings,
Shakra or Brahma Kings:

These are the small herbs.
Those who know the non outflow Dharma,
Those who can attain Nirvana,
Giving rise to Six Spiritual Penetrations
And attaining the Three Clarities,
Dwelling alone in mountain groves
Ever practicing Ch'an samadi
Attaining certification to condition-enlight-
    enment:
These are the middle-sized herbs.
Those who seek the place of the World Honored
    One
Saying, "We will become Buddhas."
Vigorously practicing concentration,
These are the superior herbs.
Further, those disciples of the Buddha
Who turn their minds to the Buddha Way
Always practising compassion
Knowing they will become Buddhas,
For sure, without doubt:
These are called the small trees.
Those who dwell in spiritual penetrations,
Turning the irreversible wheel,
Saving limitless hundreds of thousands

Of millions of living beings –
Such Bodhisattvas as these
Are called great trees.
The Buddha speaks equally,
Like the rain of a single flavor.
According to living beings' natures
They receive it differently,
Just as those herbs and trees
Each receives a different measure.
The Buddha uses this analogy
To instruct expediently.
With various phrases, he
Expounds and proclaims a single Dharma
which
In the Buddha's wisdom is
Like a drop within the sea.

Outline:

L2. Verses correlating
that which is moistened.
M1. Verses correlat-
ing praise of good
benefit and present
tranquility with uni-
versal saturation.

Commentary:

ALL LIVING BEINGS/ includes all the flying, swimming, and crawling creatures and also the vegetation. It also includes those born from wombs, those born from eggs, those born from moisture, and those born from transformation. All kinds of living beings WHO HEAR MY DHARMA/ RECEIVE IT ACCORDING TO THEIR POWER/ AND DWELL ON VARIOUS LEVELS/ They are each in a different place.

THEY MAY DWELL AMONG HUMANS OR GODS/ OR WHEEL TURNING SAGE KINGS/ There are four kinds of Wheel Turning Sage Kings: Gold, silver, bronze, and iron. The Wheel Turning Sage Kings have seven as-you-will treasures which undergo infinite changes. The inhabitants of the countries that they rule all keep the five precepts and practice the ten goods. The Gold Wheel Turning Kings watch over all four continents. The Silver Wheel Turning Kings watch over three: Purva-videha in the east, Jambudvipa in the south, Apara-godaniya in the west. They do not watch over the northern continent of Uttarakuru. The Bronze Wheel Turning Kings watch over two continents, Jambudvipa and Purva-videha. The Iron Wheel Turning King watches over only Jambudvipa. We are in Jambudvipa. If all the countries got together and picked a leader, he could be called an Iron Wheel Turning King. If the Wheel Turning Kings cultivate, their next step is Buddhahood. Shakyamuni Buddha, if he had not cultivated, would have been a Gold Wheel Turning King.

SHAKRA OR BRAHMA KINGS/ THESE ARE THE SMALL HERBS/
Such humans, gods, or other kings are called small herbs.

THOSE WHO KNOW THE NON-OUTFLOW DHARMA/ AND WHO CAN
ATTAIN NIRVANA/ GIVING RISE TO SIX SPIRITUAL PENETRATIONS/
that of the Heavenly Eye, the Heavenly Ear, the Penetration of Other's Thoughts, the Knowledge of Past Lives, the
Penetration of the Complete Spirit, and the Extinction of
Outflows, AND ATTAINING THE THREE CLARITIES/--the Clarity
of the Heavenly Eye, the Clarity of the Extinction of Outflows, the Clarity of Knowledge of Past Lives. DWELLING
ALONE IN MOUNTAIN GROVES/ They live alone in the mountains
and have practically no communication with people in the
world. They always cultivate Ch'an samadhi. The heavenly
beings are always in Ch'an samadhi. People who always
cultivate Ch'an samadhi are, for all practical purposes,
in the heavens, as well.

ATTAINING CERTIFICATION TO CONDITION-ENLIGHTENMENT:/
THESE ARE THE MIDDLE-SIZED HERBS/ Those of the Condition-
Enlightened Vehicle, one of the Two Vehicles.

THOSE WHO SEEK THE PLACE OF THE WORLD HONORED ONE/
--seek the Buddhadharma in the presence of the Buddha,
saying, "WE WILL BECOME BUDDHAS"/ VIGOROUSLY PRACTICING
CONCENTRATION/ THESE ARE THE SUPERIOR HERBS/

FURTHER, THOSE DISCIPLES OF THE BUDDHA/ WHO TURN THEIR
MINDS TO THE BUDDHA WAY/ They singlemindedly cultivate the
path of the Buddha. ALWAYS PRACTICING COMPASSION/ They
are compassionate to all beings, KNOWING THEY WILL BECOME

BUDDHAS/ FOR SURE, WITHOUT DOUBT:/ They know that they will become Buddhas. They have not the slightest doubt about it. THESE ARE CALLED THE SMALL TREES/ the Bodhisattvas.

THOSE WHO DWELL IN SPIRITUAL PENETRATIONS/ TURNING THE IRREVERSIBLE WHEEL/ of Dharma, teaching the Dharma, lecturing on the Sutras, never retiring, never resting, SAVING LIMITLESS HUNDREDS OF THOUSANDS/ OF MILLIONS OF LIVING BE-INGS/ SUCH BODHISATTVAS AS THESE/ ARE CALLED GREAT TREES/ They always turn the non-retreating Dharma wheel, thinking to teach and transform living beings. They aren't afraid of fatigue or hardship.

THE BUDDHA SPEAKS EQUALLY/ LIKE THE RAIN OF A SINGLE FLAVOR/ ACCORDING TO LIVING BEINGS NATURES/ THEY RECEIVE IT DIFFERENTLY/ The Buddha speaks the Dharma equally to all living beings, like that great cloud which rains down a single rain. He teaches living beings by means of the Buddhadharma of the One Vehicle, so that they all realize the Buddha Path. Each living being, according to its own particular nature, receives it differently. The small, middle-sized, and large herbs, and the small and large trees each receive what they should. JUST AS THOSE HERBS AND TREES/ EACH RECEIVES A DIFFERENT MEASURE/

THE BUDDHA USES THIS ANALOGY/ TO INSTRUCT EXPEDIENTLY/ WITH VARIOUS PHRASES, HE/ EXPOUNDS AND PROCLAIMS A SINGLE DHARMA WHICH/ IN THE BUDDHA'S WISDOM IS/ LIKE A DROP WITHIN THE SEA/ The Buddha uses all kinds of methods of proclaiming the wonderful Dharma of One Vehicle. However, when

you compare all of these expedient phrases and so forth to
the Buddha's wisdom, they are like a drop in the ocean.
The Buddha's wisdom is limitless and boundless. The Dharma he speaks is like a drop of water in the sea.

Sutra: T2066

I send down the rain of Dharma
Filling all the world
The Dharma of one taste is
Cultivated according to their power
Just like those forest groves
All the herbs and trees
According to their size
Grow and flourish well.
The Dharma of all the Buddhas
Is always of a single taste
It causes all the world
To attain perfection.
Through its gradual cultivation
All attain the fruits of the Way.
The Sound Hearers, those enlightened to
    conditions
Dwelling in mountain groves
Living in their final bodies
Hearing the Dharma, gain the fruit;

They are called the herbs,
And each one does grow.
If there are Bodhisattvas,
Whose wisdom is firm and solid,
Who thoroughly comprehend the triple world
And seek the supreme vehicle;
They are called small trees,
And each one does grow.
Further, those who dwell in Ch'an
Attaining spiritual powers,
Who hear the dharma of emptiness
And rejoice within their minds,
Emitting countless lights
Crossing over all beings;
They are called the large trees,
And each one does grow.

Outline:

M2. Verses correlating future
rebirth in good places and gradually entering the Way.

Commentary:

I SEND DOWN THE RAIN OF DHARMA/ The Buddha sends down
the Dharma rain. FILLING ALL THE WORLD/ It completely
fills the world, moistening all living beings. THE DHARMA

OF ONE TASTE IS/ CULTIVATED ACCORDING TO THEIR POWER/ They cultivate the One Vehicle Dharma according to their strength. JUST LIKE THOSE FOREST GROVES/ AND ALL THE HERBS AND TREES/ ACCORDING TO THEIR SIZE/ GROW AND FLOURISH WELL/ The big trees get a lot of moisture; the small trees get less.

THE DHARMA OF ALL THE BUDDHAS/ IS ALWAYS OF A SINGLE TASTE/ IT CAUSES ALL THE WORLD/ TO ATTAIN PERFECTION/ The wonderful Dharma of a Single Vehicle causes all beings in the world to perfect themselves. THROUGH ITS GRADUAL CULTIVATION/ ALL ATTAIN THE FRUITS OF THE WAY/ In the future all will realize the Way and certify to the fruit.

THE SOUND HEARERS, THOSE ENLIGHTENED TO CONDITIONS/ DWELLING IN MOUNTAIN GROVES/ LIVING IN THEIR FINAL BODIES/ HEARING THE DHARMA GAIN THE FRUIT/ THEY ARE CALLED THE HERBS/ "Final bodies" refers to certification to the Fourth Fruit of Arhatship. At this level, share-section birth and death has ended; they don't need to undergo birth and death another time. They are in their last bodies. When they hear the Buddhadharma, they gain the fruit. AND EACH ONE DOES GROW/ They each receive the share of rain they should receive; they each grow accordingly.

IF THERE ARE BODHISATTVAS/ WHOSE WISDOM IS FIRM AND SOLID/ who have great wisdom, WHO THROUGHLY COMPREHEND THE TRIPLE WORLD/ AND SEEK THE SUPREME VEHICLE/ They understand the entire triple world: The world of desire, the form world, and the formless world. These Bodhisattvas ARE CALLED SMALL TREES/ AND EACH ONE DOES GROW/

FURTHER, THOSE WHO DWELL IN CH'AN/ in Ch'an samadhi,

ATTAINING SPIRITUAL POWERS/ the Six Spiritual Powers,

WHO HEAR THE DHARMA OF EMPTINESS/ AND REJOICE WITHIN THEIR

MINDS/ They are very happy to hear that all dharmas are

but empty appearances. EMITTING COUNTLESS LIGHTS/ CROS-

SING OVER ALL BEINGS/ THEY ARE CALLED THE LARGE TREES/

AND EACH ONE DOES GROW/ They are the Great Vehicle Bodhi-

sattvas.

Sutra: T 20 b 18

In this way, Kashyapa,
The Dharma spoken by the Buddha
Is like that great cloud.
With rain of a single flavor,
It moistens all the people and flowers,
So each one bears fruit.
Kashyapa, you should know
That by using causes and conditions
And various analogies
I demonstrate and reveal the Buddha
   Path.
These are my expedients
And other Buddhas are also thus.
Now, for your sakes,

I speak of this true matter:
All of you sound hearers,
None of you have reached extinction.
What you now are walking
That is the Bodhisattva Path.
Gradually, gradually, cultivate and study,
And you'll all accomplish Buddhahood.

Outline:

> J2. Verses correlating "different
> and yet not different."

Commentary:

IN THIS WAY, KASHYAPA/ The things I have just told you about the three grasses and the two trees THE DHARMA SPOKEN BY THE BUDDHA/ IS LIKE THAT GREAT CLOUD/ The wonderful Dharma of One Vehicle is used to teach and transform living beings WITH RAIN OF A SINGLE FLAVOR/ IT MOISTENS ALL THE PEOPLE AND FLOWERS/ SO EACH ONE BEARS FRUIT/ and in the future realizes Buddhahood.

KASHYAPA, YOU SHOULD KNOW/ THAT BY USING CAUSES AND CONDITIONS/ AND VARIOUS ANALOGIES/ I DEMONSTRATE AND REVEAL THE BUDDHA PATH/ The Buddha uses all kinds of causes, conditions, and analogies to instruct living beings in the pathway to Buddhahood.

THESE ARE MY EXPEDIENTS/ AND OTHER BUDDHAS ARE ALSO

THUS/ They also employ expedient devices to teach and transform living beings. NOW, FOR YOUR SAKES/ For you, Kashyapa, I SPEAK OF THIS TRUE MATTER/ A true, real matter, the doctrine of the real teaching, and that is ALL OF YOU SOUND HEARERS/ Those of you of the Two Vehicles, that is. I said before that you had attained Nirvana, but you haven't, really. You have attained Nirvana With Residue. You have not yet attained the Nirvana Without Residue. NONE OF YOU HAVE REACHED EXTINCTION/ WHAT YOU NOW ARE WALKING/ THAT IS THE BODHISATTVA PATH/ The road you Sound Hearers are now on is the Bodhisattva Path. GRADUALLY, GRADUALLY CULTIVATE AND STUDY/ Bit by bit, go forward, day by day, forward and cultivate, and in the future YOU'LL ALL ACCOMPLISH BUDDHAHOOD/

Chapter Six : Conferring Predictions

hen the Buddha confers a prediction he tells people when in the future they will become Buddhas, what their Buddha-name and what the name of the Buddhaland will be, what their country will look like, and how long their lifespans will be. He tells them how long the Proper Dharma Age will last in that country, and how long the Dharma-Resemblance Age will last.

The Buddha confers the prediction, and one receives it. His prediction is different for each person, because each person becomes a Buddha with his own individual name. Although they are all called Buddhas, each Buddha has his own special name, just like people. Everyone has a different name. A prediction means that one is certain to become a Buddha, beyond any doubt. Once you have got your prediction, you are certain to become a Buddha. Only the Buddha can bestow predictions. So this is the Sixth Chapter of <u>The Dharma Flower Sutra</u>.

Sutra: T262 20 b26

At that time, following his expounding of the verses, the World Honored One spoke to the great assembly in this manner, "My disciple, Maha-kashyapa, in a future age will serve and behold three hundred thousand million Buddhas, World Honored Ones, making offerings, paying reverence, venerating and praising them; he will broadly proclaim the limitless Great Dharma of all the Buddhas.

Outline:

F4. Bestowing predictions.

  G1. Bestowing predictions to those of average dispositions.

    H1. Prediction for Mahakashyapa.

      I1. Prose.

        J1. Causal practice.

Commentary:

AT THAT TIME, right after Shakyamuni Buddha had finished speaking the Medicinal Herbs Chapter, FOLLOWING HIS EXPOUNDING OF THE VERSES, THE WORLD HONORED ONE SPOKE TO THE GREAT ASSEMBLY IN THIS MANNER. He announced to them, "MY DISCIPLE, MAHAKASHYAPA..." You should all recognize him. He was over a hundred years old at this time, and, is, in fact, still alive right now! He went to live in Chicken Foot Mountain in Yunnan. He's meditating in samadhi there.

"Can I see him?" you ask.

Yes, if you are sincere. If you aren't sincere, then you can't see him. Buddhism is just a question of sincerity. No matter what it is, if you are sincere, then there is a way. If you are not sincere, then there is no way.

"What should I do?"

If you are sincere, things will work out. If not, they won't. So if you want to know what to do, you should

1106

just be sincere, that's all. Be truly sincere and fear
nothing. Don't fear that people won't make offerings to
you. If no one makes offerings to you, you can end your
suffering. The reason why no one makes offerings is because in the past you cultivated wisdom and did not cultivate blessings. Need you ask?

> One who cultivates wisdom and
> neglects blessings is like an Arhat with
> an empty bowl.

No one makes offerings to him. How does one go about cultivating blessings? By practicing merit and virtue and
doing good things.

"IN A FUTURE AGE WILL SERVE AND BEHOLD THREE HUNDRED
THOUSAND MILLION BUDDHAS, WORLD HONORED ONES. He will
serve and make offerings to and reverently view all these
Buddhas. When the great officials go to see the King,
they "behold" him and report their business to him. Ma-
hakashyapa will serve and revere three hundred thousand
millions of Buddhas, World Honored Ones, MAKING OFFERINGS,
PAYING REVERENCE, VENERATING AND PRAISING THEM. HE WILL
BROADLY PROCLAIM THE LIMITLESS GREAT DHARMA OF ALL THE
BUDDHAS.

Sutra: T. 20b29
In his final body he will become a Buddha
by the name of Light Brightness Thus Come

One, one worthy of offerings, of proper and universal knowledge, one whose understanding and conduct are complete, a well-gone one who understands the world, an unsurpassed Lord, a taming and regulating hero, a teacher of gods and humans, a Buddha, a World Honored One.

Outline:

J2. Attaining the fruit.

Commentary:

"IN HIS FINAL BODY HE WILL BECOME A BUDDHA BY THE NAME OF LIGHT BRIGHTNESS THUS COME ONE, because his body will glow with golden light.

Sutra: T. 20 c 2

His country will be called Light Virtue and his aeon will be called Great Adornment.

Outline:

J3. Name of country.

Commentary:

Mahakashyapa's Buddha COUNTRY WILL BE CALLED LIGHT VIRTUE, because the people of his country will have both light and virtuous practice. The AEON WILL BE CALLED

GREAT ADORNMENT. It will be adorned by great Bodhisattvas, limitless and boundless in number.

Sutra: T. 20 c 3
His lifespan as a Buddha will last for twelve minor aeons.

Outline:

> J4. Lifespan as a Buddha.

Sutra: T. 20 c 3
The Proper Dharma will dwell there for twenty minor aeons. The Dharma Resemblance Age will also dwell there for twenty minor aeons.

Outline:

> J5. The length of the Proper and Image
> Ages of the Dharma.

Commentary:

The Dharma Resemblance Age would seem to be more or
less like the Proper Dharma Age; however, although it re-
sembles it, that is merely a resemblance.

Sutra: T. 20 c4
His realm will be adorned and free of any

*filth or evil, tiles or stones, thorns or brambles,
excrement or other impurities. The land will be
flat, without high or low places, gullys or hills.
The land will be made of lapis lazuli, and set
about with rows of jeweled trees. The roads will
be bordered with golden ropes. Precious flowers
will be scattered about, purifying it entirely.
The Bodhisattvas in that land will number in
the limitless thousands of millions, the assembly
of sound Hearers will be likewise uncountable.
No deeds of Mara will be done there, and although Mara and his subjects will exist there,
they will all protect the Buddhadharma.*

Outline:

J6. The six purities of the land.

Commentary:

"HIS REALM, the Land of Light Virtue, WILL BE ADORNED
AND FREE OF ANY FILTH OR EVIL. There will be no impurities; it will all be pure because the ground will be
made of lapis lazuli. There will be no evil karma there,
either, such as, TILES OR STONES, THORNS OR BRAMBLES, which
scratch you and tear at your clothing. If you're not
careful, they can draw blood. EXCREMENT, the people will
not go to the bathroom. This is a mark of Ch'an samadhi.

THE LAND WILL BE FLAT, WITHOUT HIGH OR LOW PLACES, GULLYS

OR HILLS. THE LAND WILL BE MADE OF LAPIS LAZULI AND SET

ABOUT WITH ROWS OF JEWELED TREES, trees adorned with the

seven jewels. THE ROADS WILL BE BORDERED WITH GOLDEN

ROPES, like railings. PRECIOUS FLOWERS WILL BE SCATTERED

ABOUT in the country all the time. PURIFYING IT ENTIRELY.

All places in it will be clean and pure.

THE BODHISATTVAS IN THAT LAND WILL NUMBER IN THE

LIMITLESS THOUSANDS OF MILLIONS. There will be very many

great Bodhisattvas adorning this land. THE ASSEMBLY OF

SOUND HEARERS WILL BE LIKEWISE UNCOUNTABLE. NO DEEDS OF

MARA WILL BE DONE THERE. There will be no demonic ob-

stacles, which means that there will be no affliction,

because in that land the people will always be cultivat-

ing Ch'an samadhi. Because they have samadhi power, the

deeds of Mara vanish. ALTHOUGH MARA AND HIS SUBJECTS

WILL EXIST THERE, ALL WILL PROTECT THE BUDDHADHARMA. They

may be demons, but here they will protect the Buddhadharma;

they won't try to ruin the Buddhadharma. Why is this?

This is because the Patriarch Kashyapa cultivated a lot

of ascetic practices, and so he was victorious over all

the demonic hoardes. He has subdued them all, thus they

have become Dharma Protectors. Why do cultivators prac-

tice asceticism? Because through it one can turn the de-

mons into Dharma Protectors. If you cultivate and truly

have a measure of attainment, the demons will come to test

you out. In the future, these same demons will be your

best Dharma Protectors. If you have no measure of attainment in your cultivation, the demons will remain demons,
and they will not turn into Dharma protectors.

Sutra: T 20 c 9
At that time, the World Honored One, wishing
to restate this principle, spoke verses saying,
I declare to the Bhikshus that
By using my Buddha Eye
I see that Kashyapa
In a future age
Countless aeons from now
Shall become a Buddha
And that in the future he
Shall make offerings to, revere and behold
Three hundred ten thousands of millions
Of Buddhas, World Honored Ones.
And, for the sake of the Buddha's wisdom
He shall purely cultivate Brahman conduct.
He shall make offerings to the highest
Honored One, doubly complete and then
Cultivate and practice all
Unsurpassed Wisdom.
In his final body

He shall become a Buddha.

Outline:

>> I2. Verse

>>> J1. Causal practice, resulting frui-
>>> tion.

Commentary:

AT THAT TIME, THE WORLD HONORED ONE, Shakyamuni Buddha, WISHING TO RESTATE THIS PRINCIPLE, SPOKE VERSES,
SAYING.

I DECLARE TO THE BHIKSHUS THAT/ He told the Bhikshus and the Bhikshunis. Now, there were also laypeople
present, Bodhisattvas, Sound Hearers, Arhats, gods and
dragons of the eightfold division, whom he also addressed.

BY USING MY BUDDHA EYE/ to contemplate, I SEE THAT
KASHYAPA/ IN A FUTURE AGE/ COUNTLESS AEONS FROM NOW/
SHALL BECOME A BUDDHA/ Who knows how long that will be?
AND THAT IN THE FUTURE HE/ SHALL MAKE OFFERINGS TO, RE-
VERE, AND BEHOLD/ Before he becomes a Buddha he will
make offerings to THREE HUNDRED TEN THOUSANDS OF MIL-
LIONS/ OF BUDDHAS, WORLD HONORED ONES/

AND, FOR THE SAKE OF THE BUDDHA'S WISDOM/ Why does
he make such offerings? Why is he so reverent? Because
he seeks the Buddha's wisdom. That is why HE SHALL MAKE
OFFERINGS TO THE HIGHEST/ HONORED ONE, DOUBLY COMPLETE,
AND THEN/ The Buddha is doubly complete in blessings and

wisdom.   CULTIVATE AND PRACTICE ALL/ UNSURPASSED WISDOM/
The highest wisdom, IN HIS FINAL BODY/ HE SHALL BECOME
A BUDDHA/ He will realize Buddhahood.

Sutra : T. 20 c 17
   His land will be pure,
   With lapis lazuli for soil,
   And with many jeweled trees
   Lining the roadways,
   And with the roads set off by golden cords,
   Delighting all who see it.
   Fine fragrance will always issue forth,
   Rare flowers will be strewn about;
   With all manner of rare articles
   It shall be adorned.
   The land will be flat and even
   Without hills or gullys.
   The assembly of Bodhisattvas
   Will be unreckonable.
   Their minds will be gentle
   Having gained great spiritual powers;
   They will reverently uphold the Buddha's
   Great Vehicle sutras.
   The assembly of Sound Hearers,
   Without outflows, in their last bodies,

Sons of the Dharma King,
will also be beyond all count.
So that, even with the Heavenly Eye,
Their number shall not be known.

Outline:

J2. Verses of purity of the land.

Commentary:

HIS LAND WILL BE PURE/ WITH LAPIS LAZULI FOR SOIL/
Because he cultivated pure ascetic practices in the cause
ground, as a result, the soil of his land will be made
of lapis lazuli. AND WITH MANY JEWELED TREES/ LINING
THE ROADWAYS/ AND WITH THE ROADS SET OFF BY GOLDEN CORDS/
DELIGHTING ALL WHO SEE IT/ FINE FRAGRANCE WILL ALWAYS
ISSUE FORTH/ Both the people and the country itself will
always issue a fine scent. Both the Dependent and the
Proper Retribution Worlds, then, will be fragrant. RARE
FLOWERS WILL BE STREWN ABOUT/ heavenly maidens will con-
stantly toss flowers from the sky WITH ALL MANNER OF RARE
ARTICLES/ IT SHALL BE ADORNED/

THE LAND WILL BE FLAT/ Why? Because in the cause
ground, Mahakashyapa cultivated his mind-ground until it
was level and even. Consequently, his Buddhaland will
also be level and even. WITHOUT HILLS OR GULLYS/ Because,
in the cause ground, Mahakashyapa practiced equal compassion, his Buddhaland is level, too, without mountains or

crevices.

THE ASSEMBLY OF BODHISATTVAS/ WILL BE UNRECKONABLE/ No one will be able to count them. No one will know where they came from; no one will know where they are going! There will be so many of them, they won't even recognize each other! If, with their wisdom, they can't even keep each other's names straight, how much the less will anyone else be able to keep track of them!

THEIR MINDS WILL BE GENTLE/ HAVING GAINED GREAT SPIRITUAL POWERS/ The Five Eyes and Six Spiritual Penetrations. THEY WILL REVERENTLY UPHOLD THE BUDDHA'S/ GREAT VEHICLE SUTRAS/ THE ASSEMBLY OF SOUND HEARERS/ WITHOUT OUTFLOWS, IN THEIR LAST BODIES/ SONS OF THE DHARMA KING/ the Buddha, WILL ALSO BE BEYOND ALL COUNT/ SO THAT, EVEN WITH THE HEAVENLY EYE/ THEIR NUMBER SHALL NOT BE KNOWN/ Even if you use your Heavenly Eye, you won't be able to count them.

Sutra: T. 20 c 27

His lifespan as a Buddha will be
Twelve minor aeons, and
His Proper Dharma will dwell in the world
Twenty minor aeons.
The Dharma Image Age will dwell
Also for twenty minor aeons.

1116

Outline:

J4. The Proper and Image Ages.

Commentary:

HIS LIFESPAN AS A BUDDHA WILL BE/ TWELVE MINOR AEONS,
AND/ HIS PROPER DHARMA WILL DWELL IN THE WORLD/ TWENTY
MINOR AEONS/ THE DHARMA IMAGE AGE WILL DWELL/ ALSO FOR
TWELVE MINOR AEONS/

Sutra: T. 20 c 27
*The World Honored One, Light Brightness
Shall have a history such as this.*

Outline:

J5. Conclusion.

Commentary:

THE WORLD HONORED ONE/ the Thus Come One, LIGHT
BRIGHTNESS/ SHALL HAVE A HISTORY SUCH AS THIS/

His Buddhaland will be called Light Virtue, but you
shouldn't think that this is just ordinary light. It is
the light of wisdom, the virtue of Prajna, and the virtue
of offering up all good conduct. In his land everyone
will be wise and intelligent. There won't be a single
confused person there. Everyone's minds will always be
pure and manifesting wisdom. They will never be stupid.
Everyone will have wisdom and virtuous conduct.

Sutra: T. 20 c 28

At that time, Mahamaudgalyayana, Subhuti and Mahakatyayana were very agitated. They singlemindedly joined their palms, gazed upward at the World Honored One, not lowering their gaze for a moment, and with a single voice spoke these verses:

Outline:

> H2. Predictions for three Arhats.
>
> > I1. Request.
> >
> > > J1. Request Proper.

Commentary:

AT THAT TIME, right after Shakyamuni Buddha had bestowed a prediction upon Mahakashyapa, MAHAMAUDGALYAYANA, SUBHUTI, AND MAHAKATYAYANA WERE VERY AGITATED/ They were all very nervous. "The Buddha gave Mahakashyapa a prediction! What about us? Will we get one? Do we have to ask for one?" They couldn't wait any longer, so Mahamaudgalyayana, foremost in spiritual powers, SUBHUTI, foremost at understanding emptiness, and Mahakatyayana, foremost in debate, were very agitated and upset. They weren't exactly afraid, but their hair was standing on end. "Mahakashyapa got a prediction! What about us? Will we pass the test? Will we get our degrees?" They were very nervous. Then, they managed to calm down somewhat and SINGLE-MINDEDLY JOINED THEIR PALMS in respect, GAZED UPWARD AT THE WORLD HONORED ONE, NOT LOWERING THEIR GAZE FOR A MOMENT, not blinking, like their eyes had entered samadhi and couldn't move! I've seen a lot of Americans do this. They stare at each other. Chinese don't do that. They don't consider it polite. If you stare at them, they might think you were crazy. AND WITH A SINGLE VOICE SPOKE THESE VERSES:

Sutra: T. 21a2

Great brave hero, the World Honored One,
The Shakyan Dharma King,
Out of pity for us all
Bestow the Buddha Word!

GREAT, BRAVE HERO, THE WORLD HONORED ONE/ The Buddha is a hero both in and beyond the world. THE SHAKYAN DHARMA KING/ King of the Dharma, born of the Shakyan clan. OUT OF PITY FOR US ALL/ all living beings, BESTOW THE BUDDHA WORD!

Sutra: T. 21a3

If, knowing our profoundest thoughts,
You see that we gain predictions,
It will be like a sprinkling of sweet dew,
Dispelling heat and giving cool refreshment.

*It'll be like a person from a famine-stricken
    land,
Who suddenly encounters a royal feast:
His mind holds doubt and fear,
And he doesn't dare go ahead and eat.
But, if he gained the king's permission,
Then he would certainly dare to eat.*

Outline:

J2. Setting up parable.

Commentary:

IF, KNOWING OUR PROFOUNDEST THOUGHTS/ World Honored
One, you should know what's deep in our minds. YOU SEE
THAT WE GAIN PREDICTIONS/ IT WILL BE LIKE A SPRINKLING
OF SWEET DEW/ DISPELLING HEAT AND GIVING COOL REFRESH-
MENT/

IT'LL BE LIKE A PERSON FROM A FAMINE-STRICKEN LAND/
WHO SUDDENLY ENCOUNTERS A ROYAL FEAST/ a great king's
banquet! HIS MIND HOLDS DOUBT AND FEAR/ AND HE DOESN'T
DARE GO AHEAD AND EAT/ BUT, IF HE GAINED THE KING'S PER-
MISSION/ THEN HE WOULD CERTAINLY DARE TO EAT/

Sutra: T. 21a9
*We, in the same way, ever think
Of the errors of the Small Vehicle*

And do not know how we are
To gain the Buddha's unsurpassed wisdom.
Although we hear the Buddha's voice
Saying that we shall become Buddhas,
Our minds hold worry and fear,
Like one who dares not yet to eat.
If we were favored by the Buddha's pre-
   diction,
Then we should be happy and at peace.

Outline:

J3. Correlation with Dharma.

Commentary:

WE IN THE SAME WAY, EVER THINK/ OF THE ERRORS OF THE
SMALL VEHICLE/ We keep thinking how we have the Small Ve-
hicle disposition. AND DO NOT KNOW HOW WE ARE/ TO GAIN
THE BUDDHA'S UNSURPASSED WISDOM/ ALTHOUGH WE HEAR THE
BUDDHA'S VOICE/ SAYING THAT WE SHALL BECOME BUDDHAS/ OUR
MINDS HOLD WORRY AND FEAR/ LIKE ONE WHO DARES NOT YET TO
EAT/ We don't quite believe it, you know. We are so small
and petty, we of the Small Vehicle. Can we really become
Buddhas?

IF WE WERE FAVORED BY THE BUDDHA'S PREDICTION/ See
how nervous they are? Kashyapa got one! Now we want predictions, too! THEN WE SHOULD BE HAPPY AND AT PEACE/

Sutra: T. 21 a 14

Great, brave hero, World Honored One,
You who always wish peace for the world
Please bestow predictions upon us
Like giving the famished permission to eat!

Outline:

> J4. Conclusion of request.

Commentary:

GREAT, BRAVE HERO, WORLD HONORED ONE/ YOU WHO ALWAYS WISH PEACE FOR THE WORLD/ to bring peace to all living beings, PLEASE BESTOW PREDICTIONS UPON US/"We can't wait any longer!! Please hurry and tell us. Can we become Buddhas? Do we have a chance? Aren't we about the same as Mahakashyapa? He got one. Shouldn't we, er...we hope you'll hurry and give us one!" LIKE GIVING THE FAMISHED PERMISSION TO EAT!/ to partake of the royal feast. Otherwise, we might die of hunger! Our stomachs might stage a revolution!

Sutra: T. 21 a 16

At that time, the World Honored One, knowing the thoughts in the minds of his great disciples, told the Bhikshus, "Subhuti will in a future age serve and behold three hundreds of myriads of millions of nayutas of Buddhas,

*making offerings, paying reverence, venerating,
and praising them, ever cultivating the Brahman conduct, and perfecting the Bodhisattva
Way.*

Outline:

> I2. Bestowing predictions.
>> J1. Predictions for Subhuti.
>>> K1. Prose.
>>>> L1. Causal practice.

Commentary:

AT THAT TIME, after the three great disciples had
asked in verse to receive predictions, THE WORLD HONORED
ONE, KNOWING THE THOUGHTS IN THE MINDS OF HIS GREAT DIS-
CIPLES. He knew exactly what was on their minds. The
Vajra Sutra says, "The Buddha fully knows and sees all
the thoughts in the minds of all beings." Living beings
have various thoughts which the Buddha fully knows.

TOLD THE BHIKSHUS, in the Dharma Assembly, "SUBHUTI,
'Born-of-Emptiness,' WILL, IN A FUTURE AGE, SERVE AND BE-
HOLD THREE HUNDREDS OF MYRIADS OF MILLIONS OF NAYUTAS
OF BUDDHAS, MAKING OFFERINGS, of the ten kinds of offer-
ings: incense, flowers, lamps, beads, canopies, banners,
clothing, food and fruit, music, and joined palms, PAYING
REVERENCE, VENERATING, AND PRAISING THEM, EVER-CULTIVAT-

ING BRAHMAN CONDUCT, AND PERFECTING THE BODHISATTVA WAY,

the Six Perfections and Ten Thousand Practices.

Sutra : T. 21a 19

In his final body, he will become a Buddha called Name Appearance Thus Come One, one worthy of offerings, of proper and universal knowledge, one whose understanding and conduct are complete, a well-gone one who understands the world, an unsurpassed lord, a taming and regulating hero, teacher of gods and humans, Buddha, World Honored One.

Outline:

> L2. Obtaining the
>
> fruition.

Commentary:

"IN HIS FINAL BODY, Subhuti WILL BECOME A BUDDHA CALLED NAME-APPEARANCE. Subhuti was foremost in understanding emptiness. Knowing the emptiness of Dharmas is knowing the emptiness of names and appearances. So, as a Buddha he will be called "Name Appearance" THUS COME ONE. Riding on the Way which is "Thus," he "Comes" to realize right enlightenment. ONE WORTHY OF OFFERINGS, from gods and humans, one of PROPER AND UNIVERSAL KNOW-

LEDGE. Knowing that the mind produces the ten thousand dharmas and that the ten thousand Dharmas are only the mind, ONE WHOSE UNDERSTANDING AND CONDUCT ARE COMPLETE, the light of his wisdom and cultivation are complete. A WELL-GONE ONE WHO UNDERSTANDS THE WORLD, UNSURPASSED LORD, there is no one higher, A TAMING AND REGULATING HERO, subduing living beings in the three realms, TEACHER OF GODS AND HUMANS, beings in the three realms, BUDDHA..."

What is a Buddha? Let's review: The Buddha is just a person, and people are just Buddhas. But the Buddha's a Buddha and people are people. The Buddha was a person who cultivated and then became a Buddha. If people cultivate, they can become Buddhas. If they do not cultivate, they can't. You can't fail to cultivate and claim to be a Buddha. If in the beginning the Buddha hadn't cultivated, he wouldn't have become a Buddha, either.

How does one cultivate? First of all, wake up! This means, you yourself must wake up. It doesn't mean that you go demanding that other people wake up. The Buddha is awake, enlightened; living beings are confused. If you wake up, then you are a Buddha among living beings. While you are confused, you are a living being among Buddhas. Awakening, or enlightenment, just means that you gain true understanding. There are three kinds of enlightenment:

1. Self-enlightenment: This distinguishes the Buddha from common, unenlightened people. They are unenlightened.

Unenlightened to what? To the fact that they have faults and bad karma. It's a lucky thing that the karma we have created has no physical shape. If it did, it would be big enough to break right through the entirety of empty space! It may not have a shape, so we don't have to worry about storing it anywhere, but it's still there; it never leaves you for a moment. The Buddha is enlightened, and so he is different from common people. Gaining enlightenment for oneself, however, is not establishing merit and virtue. Since the Buddha wants to set up merit, he goes on to teach others.

2. Enlightening Others. He uses the methods and principles he employed to gain enlightenment and teaches them to others, enlightening them all so that everyone can get enlightened together. This is the practice of the Bodhisattva path. It makes the Buddha different from those of the Small Vehicle who only care to enlighten themselves.

3. Perfection of enlightenment and practice. This means that the Buddha has perfected his own enlightenment and perfected the practice of bringing enlightenment to others.

These are the three kinds of enlightenment. We say,

> Having perfected three kinds of enlightenment
> and ten thousand virtues,
> He is, therefore, called a "Buddha."

1126

WORLD HONORED ONE, the most venerable one in the
world and beyond the world.

Sutra: T. 21 a 21

His aeon will be called Possessing-Jewels. His country will be called Giving Birth to Jewels, his land will be level, with crystal for soil, and jeweled trees for adornments. It will be without hills or gullys, stones, thorns, filth or excrement. Jeweled flowers will cover the ground, purifying it entirely. The people of his land will all dwell on jeweled terraces or in precious, fine towers. The assembly of Sound Hearers will be limitless and boundless, so that they cannot be known by resort to number or analogy. The assembly of Bodhisattvas will number in the countless thousands of myriads of millions of nayutas .

Outline:

> L3. Aeons, land, and
> adornments.

Commentary:

"Name Appearance Thus Come One will appear in an AEON called POSSESSING-JEWELS. What jewels? The Triple Jewel

of the Buddha, Dharma, and Sangha. HIS COUNTRY WILL BE
CALLED GIVING BIRTH TO JEWELS, because the Triple Jewel
will arise there. HIS LAND WILL BE LEVEL. Why? Because
Subhuti cultivated his mind ground until it was level.
WITH CRYSTAL FOR SOIL. The light of the wisdom Subhuti
cultivated gives him crystal soil in his Buddhaland. AND
JEWELED TREES FOR ADORNMENTS. They grow naturally in his
land. IT WILL BE WITHOUT HILLS OR GULLYS, STONES, THORNS,
FILTH, OR EXCREMENT. There will be nothing unclean there.
JEWELED FLOWERS WILL COVER THE GROUND, PURIFYING IT EN-
TIRELY. The entire land will be clean. THE PEOPLE OF
HIS LAND WILL ALL DWELL ON JEWELED TERRACES, made of the
seven gems, OR IN PRECIOUS, FINE, TOWERS.

THE ASSEMBLY OF SOUND HEARERS WILL BE LIMITLESS AND
BOUNDLESS, SO THAT THEY CANNOT BE KNOWN BY RESORT TO NUM-
BER OR ANALOGY. THE ASSEMBLY OF BODHISATTVAS WILL NUMBER
IN THE COUNTLESS THOUSANDS OF MYRIADS OF MILLIONS OF NA-
YUTAS.

Sutra: T. 21 a 26
*His lifespan as a Buddha will last for twelve
minor aeons.*

Outline:

L4. Lifespan.

Commentary:

"HIS LIFESPAN AS A BUDDHA WILL LAST FOR TWELVE MINOR
AEONS. He will live as a Buddha for twelve minor aeons.

Sutra: T. 21 a 26

The Proper Dharma will dwell there for twenty minor aeons. The Dharma Image Age will also dwell there for twenty minor aeons. This Buddha will constantly dwell in empty space, speaking Dharma for the multitudes and crossing over limitless Bodhisattvas and Sound Hearers.

Outline:

> L5. Proper and
> Image Ages.

Commentary:

"THE PROPER DHARMA Age will endure for twenty small
aeons, and THE DHARMA IMAGE AGE will last for just as
long. THIS BUDDHA, Name Appearance Thus Come One, WILL
CONSTANTLY DWELL IN EMPTY SPACE, this represents the emptiness of the Primary Principle, SPEAKING DHARMA FOR THE
MULTITUDES AND CROSSING OVER LIMITLESS BODHISATTVAS AND
SOUND HEARERS.

Sutra: T. 21 a 29

At that time the World Honored One, wishing
to restate this principle spoke verses saying,
Assembled Bhikshus
I shall now tell you,
Listen singlemindedly
To what I'm going to say.

Outline:

> K2. Verse.
>> L1. Admonishment
>> to listen.

Sutra: T. 21 a 29

My great disciple,
Subhuti,
Will become a Buddha
Called Name-Appearance.
After making offerings to countless
Myriads of millions of Buddhas
Following the Buddhas' practices,
He will gradually perfect the Great Way.
In his final body he shall
Obtain thirty two marks,
Upright and beautiful

1130

Like a jeweled mountain.

Outline:

> L2. Causal prac-
> tice and result-
> ing fruition.

Commentary:

Everyone was warned! They'd better listen well!! Don't have false thinking; don't fall asleep. "MY GREAT DISCIPLE, here, my finest disciple, really good disciple, Subhuti." Everyone knows that he had three names. First, he was called "Empty-born" because, when he was born, all the treasures disappeared from his father's one hundred and eight treasuries! Naturally, his father was rather nervous about this, wondering where they went. Had they been stolen? He went to a diviner to find out what had happened, and the diviner said that the whole thing was extremely auspicious. Hearing this, his father gave him the name "Good and Lucky." After a week, all the treasures reappeared in his father's one hundred and eight treasuries, and he was given the name, "Good Appearance." The Buddha was quite fond of Subhuti and paid a lot of attention to him... WILL BECOME A BUDDHA. Don't look down on him. He's going to become a Buddha, you realize. CALLED NAME-APPEARANCE/ His Buddha name will be Name Appearance Thus Come One. AFTER MAKING OFFERINGS TO COUNT-

LESS/ MYRIADS OF MILLIONS OF BUDDHAS/ FOLLOWING THE BUD-
DHA'S PRACTICES/ Why will he become a Buddha? This is
very important. Because he follows the Buddha's practices and practices just as the Buddha does. Whatever
the Buddha does, he does. He practices just as the Buddha does and doesn't attempt to set himself up as different or better than the Buddha. HE WILL GRADUALLY PER-
FECT THE GREAT WAY/ The word "gradual" is important here.
You shouldn't think, "Oh, I can't cultivate. I can't get
rid of my faults!" and get all nervous about it. "My desire makes me nervous." Don't be nervous. Work on it
gradually. You have to work, and you have to cultivate,
yes, but you shouldn't get confused about it. The more
confused you are, the more confused you'll get. If you
wake up, you are following the Buddha. If you don't wake
up, you are following confusion, not the Buddha. So you
see, Subhuti will cultivate and gradually become a Buddha.
He will cultivate during the time of three hundred myriads
of millions of Buddhas. How long do you think that took?
A Buddha doesn't necessarily appear every aeon, even. He
will make offerings to that many Buddhas and, day by day,
cultivate until he reaches his goal. IN HIS FINAL BODY
HE SHALL/ In his last body, practicing the Bodhisattva
Way, he will OBTAIN THE THRITY-TWO MARKS and eighty minor
characteristics. We also cultivate in order to attain
the thirty-two marks. A Buddha has these marks and is
beautifully adorned in blessings, UPRIGHT AND BEAUTIFUL/

LIKE A JEWELED MOUNTAIN/ Everyone who sees him will honor
him.

Sutra: T. 21b6
　His Buddha land will be
　Foremost in purity and adornment.
　Living beings who see it
　All will take delight in it.
　And as a Buddha therein
　He will save limitless multitudes.
　Within his Buddha Dharma
　Will be many Bodhisattvas,
　All of sharp faculties,
　Turning the non-retreating wheel.
　This land will ever be
　Adorned with Bodhisattvas;
　The assembly of Sound Hearers
　Will be beyond all reckoning.
　All having gained the Three Clarities,
　And perfected the Six Spiritual powers
　Abiding in the Eight Liberations
　And possessing great awesome virtue.
　When this Buddha speaks the Dharma
　He will manifest limitless

Spiritual powers and transformations,
Inconceivable.
The people, both gods and humans,
Their numbers like the Ganges sands,
All will join their palms
To hear and accept that Buddha's words.

Outline:

L3. Verse of pur-
ity of land.

Commentary:

HIS BUDDHALAND WILL BE/ FOREMOST IN PURITY AND ADORN-
MENT/ The Buddhaland of Name Appearance Thus Come One is
adorned and pure. LIVING BEINGS WHO SEE IT/ who go there,
ALL WILL TAKE DELIGHT IN IT/ They will really like it.

AND AS A BUDDHA THEREIN/ HE WILL SAVE LIMITLESS MUL-
TITUDES/ limitless, countless living beings. WITHIN HIS
BUDDHADHARMA/ WILL BE MANY BODHISATTVAS/ ALL OF SHARP FAC-
ULTIES/ TURNING THE NON-RETREATING WHEEL/ They will all
be extremely intelligent. They will turn the Dharma
wheel, to teach and transform living beings and purify
the Buddhalands.

HIS LAND WILL EVER BE/ ADORNED WITH BODHISATTVAS/
THE ASSEMBLY OF SOUND HEARERS/ WILL BE BEYOND ALL RECKON-
ING/ ALL HAVING GAINED THE THREE CALRITIES/ the heavenly

eye, the knowledge of past lives, the extinction of out-
flows. AND PERFECTED THE SIX SPIRITUAL POWERS/ ABIDING
IN THE EIGHT LIBERATIONS/ AND POSSESSING GREAT AWESOME
VIRTUE/

    WHEN THIS BUDDHA SPEAKS THE DHARMA/ HE WILL MANI-
FEST LIMITLESS/ SPIRITUAL POWERS AND TRANSFORMATIONS/
INCONCEIVABLE/

    THE PEOPLE, BOTH GODS AND HUMANS/ THEIR NUMBERS LIKE
THE GANGES SANDS/ ALL WILL JOIN THEIR PALMS/ TO HEAR AND
ACCEPT THAT BUDDHA'S WORDS/

Sutra: T. 21 b15
That Buddha's lifespan will be Twelve minor aeons,

Outline:

L4. Lifespan.

Commentary:

    THAT BUDDHA'S LIFESPAN WILL BE/ The Buddha, Name
Appearance, will live for TWELVE MINOR AEONS/

Sutra: T. 21 b15
The Proper Dharma will dwell in the world For twenty minor aeons; The Dharma Resemblance Age will dwell For twenty minor aeons, also.

Outline:

L5. Proper and

Dharma Image Ages.

Commentary:

THE PROPER DHARMA WILL DWELL IN THE WORLD/ FOR TWENTY MINOR AEONS/ THE DHARMA RESEMBLANCE AGE WILL DWELL/ FOR TWENTY MINOR AEONS/

Sutra: T. 21 b 17

At that time, the World Honored One further addressed the assembly of Bhikshus saying, "I will now tell you: In a future age, Mahakatyayana will make offerings of various articles to, and will reverently serve eight thousand million Buddhas, honoring and venerating them. After the extinction of those Buddhas, he will erect a stupa for each, one thousand yojanas in height, five hundred yojanas in breadth, and made of the seven jewels: gold, silver, lapis lazuli, mother of pearl, carnelian, pearls, and agate. He will make offerings of many flowers, beaded necklaces, paste incense, powdered incense, burning incense, silk canopies and banners *to the stupa. After that, he will further make offerings to twenty thousand million Buddhas in the same manner. Having made offerings to those Buddhas, he will perfect the Bodhisattva Way.*

Outline:

> J2. Prediction for Maha-
> katyayana.
>
>> K1. Prose.
>>
>>> L1. Causal prac-
>>> tice.

Commentary:

AT THAT TIME, right after Subhuti had received his prediction, THE WORLD HONORED ONE FURTHER ADDRESSED THE ASSEMBLY OF BHIKSHUS, SAYING, "I WILL NOW TELL YOU something. Relax, and pay close attention. IN A FUTURE AGE, MAHAKATYAYANA, whose name means literary elegance because he is such an accomplished writer and foremost of the Buddha's disciples in debate, WILL MAKE OFFERINGS OF VARIOUS ARTICLES TO, AND WILL REVERENTLY SERVE, EIGHT THOUSAND MILLION BUDDHAS. Articles refers to things one can offer to the Buddha, like lamps, flowers, flower vases, and so on. HONORING AND VERNERATING THEM, with his body-karma, he will honor the Buddhas, and with his mouth-karma he will venerate and praise them.

AFTER THE EXTINCTION OF THOSE BUDDHAS, HE WILL ERECT
A STUPA FOR EACH, ONE THOUSAND YOJANAS IN HEIGHT. In the
future, we will build a stupa to hold the relics of the
Venerable Master Hsü Lao. Although we didn't meet up with
the Buddha appearing in the world, Master Hsü Lao, such
a great Bodhisattva, was here, and we should make a stupa
to honor him. FIVE HUNDRED YOJANAS IN BREADTH. A large
yojana is 80 miles, a middle-sized yojana is 60 miles,
and a small yojana is 40 miles. AND MADE OF THE SEVEN
JEWELS: GOLD, SILVER, LAPIS LAZULI, MOTHER-OF-PEARL,
CARNEILIAN, PEARLS, AND AGATE. HE WILL MAKE OFFERINGS OF
MANY FLOWERS, BEADED NECKLACES, PASTE INCENSE, POWDERED
INCENSE, BURNING INCENSE, SILK CANOPIES, AND BANNERS TO
THE STUPA.

AFTER THAT, HE WILL FURTHER MAKE OFFERINGS TO TWENTY
THOUSAND MILLION BUDDHAS IN THE SAME MANNER. HAVING MADE
OFFERINGS TO THOSE BUDDHAS, HE WILL PERFECT THE BODHISAT-
TVA WAY.

Sutra: T. 21b24
*He will then become a Buddha called Jam-
bunada Gold Light Thus Come One, one worthy
of offerings, of proper and universal knowledge,
one whose understanding and conduct are complete, a well-gone one who understands the*

world, unsurpassed lord, a taming and reg-
ulating hero, teacher of gods and humans,
Buddha World Honored One.

Outline:

L2. Attaining

the Fruit.

Commentary:

"HE WILL THEN BECOME A BUDDHA CALLED JAMBUNADA GOLD
LIGHT THUS COME ONE." "Jambu" is the name of a tree.
"Nada" means "continent." This is the Southern Continent,
the one we live in. In this continent there is a tree
called the Jambu Tree. It is said that when this tree
bears its glistening fruit, the fruit falls into the river and turns the sand into gold. Other people say that
the fruit itself turns into gold. Still others say that
the leaves turn into gold when they fall in the river.

So, this Buddha's name was Jambunanda Gold Light
Thus Come One, because his wisdom-light made him extreme-
ly sharp and invincible. WORTHY OF OFFERINGS, OF PROPER
AND UNIVERSAL KNOWLEDGE, ONE WHOSE UNDERSTANDING AND CON-
DUCT ARE COMPLETE. A WELL-GONE ONE WHO UNDERSTANDS THE
WORLD, UNSURPASSED LORD, A TAMING AND REGULATING HERO,
TEACHER OF GODS AND MEN, BUDDHA, WORLD HONORED ONE.

Sutra: T. 21 b 26

The land will be flat and even with crystal for soil and jeweled trees as adorments. The roads will be bordered with golden ropes, and the ground covered with fine flowers, purifying it entirely, so that those who see it are delighted. The four evil paths will not exist there, that is, the hells, hungry ghosts, animals, and asuras. There will many gods, humans, assembled Sound Hearers and Bodhisattvas who will number in the limitless myriads of millions, and all adorning that land.

Outline:

> L3. Purity of the
>
> lands.

Commentary:

"THE LAND WILL BE FLAT AND EVEN, WITH CRYSTAL FOR SOIL, because in the past he cultivated and leveled the mind-ground, in the result, his Buddhaland, the dependent retribution world, will be level. AND JEWELED TREES AS ADORNMENTS, trees made up of the seven jewels. THE ROADS WILL BE BORDERED WITH GOLDEN ROPES." We make rail-

ings out of metal or wood, but in Katyayana's Buddha land
they will be made of gold. "AND THE GROUND COVERED WITH
FINE FLOWERS, PURIFYING IT ENTIRELY. The heavenly maidens will scatter heavenly flowers, covering the ground.
When the petals wilt and fall, a light breeze will blow
them away, and new buds will fall. PURIFYING IT ENTIRELY.
It is purified because in the causal ground this Buddha
did no evil and offered up all good conduct. SO THAT
THOSE WHO SEE IT ARE DELIGHTED. All who see this country
--to say nothing of seeing this Buddha--will be happy.
THE FOUR EVIL PATHS WILL NOT EXIST THERE, THAT IS, THE
HELLS. Where do the hells come from? Hatred. If you
have no hatred, then there are no hells. If you wonder
whether or not you are going to fall into the hells, ask
yourself whether or not you are hateful. If you are hateful, then you have a line into the hells. HUNGRY GHOSTS.
Where do they come from? Greed. If you are greedy, you
can turn into a ghost. For example, if you always want
to eat and can never get your fill and just think about
eating all the time, in the future you may turn into a
hungry ghost. Since you were so afraid of going hungry,
you may just turn into a hungry ghost!

How does one turn into an ANIMAL? By being stupid.
Why are you stupid? Out of ignorance. So, those who
study the Buddhadharma should never be jealous of others.
Don't be jealous of others' beauty. If you are jealous
of the way they look, you will become even uglier. The

more jealous you are, the wierder you will look, until
you don't even look human anymore. Ugly people should
return the light and realize that they are ugly because
they were jealous of others in the past.

If someone is smarter than you, if they remember all
the Sutras and teachings after hearing them only once,
take care that you don't get jealous. Don't be jealous
of their good memories. The more jealous you are, the
stupider you'll get. Some people see others cultivating
the Way, and they get very upset. "Hey! Look at that
little novice. He recites and bows and kneels there all
day. He works so hard..." If you are jealous of him,
you won't be able to cultivate in the future. Why not?
Because you were jealous. Why can't you get any samadhi
power? Because you are jealous. It doesn't matter
whether you are working or going to school, or whatever,
just don't be jealous. You should hope that others are
better than you. That's the resolve of the Bodhisattva.
If you hope that others are not as good as you are, that's
the resolve of a demon! a ghost! and an animal!

If you see everyone as a Buddha, then you are a Buddha. If you see everyone as an asura, then you're an
asura. So, don't look at others' faults.

ASURAS are beings who are hostile and like to fight.
They insist on fighting with everyone. In our present-
day world, people fight with people, families fight with
families, and nations battle nations. This is the age

of the asura. In this Buddha's land, the Four Evil Ways
will not exist. "THERE WILL BE MANY GODS, HUMANS, ASSEM-
BLED SOUND HEARERS, of the Small Vehicle, AND BODHISAT-
TVAS who practice the Bodhisattva Path, teaching and
transforming all living beings, pruifying Buddha lands,
WHO WILL NUMBER IN THE LIMITLESS MYRIADS OF MILLIONS AND
ADORN THAT LAND."

Sutra: T. 21c1

His lifespan as a Buddha will be twelve minor aeons.

Outline:

L4. Lifespan.

Commentary:

"His life as a Buddha will last TWELVE MINOR AEONS."

Sutra: T. 21c2

His Proper Dharma will dwell in the world twenty minor aeons. The Dharma Resemblance Age will dwell also for twenty minor aeons.

Outline:

L5. Proper and
Image Ages.

Commentary:

"The PROPER DHARMA will last twenty minor aeons, and then the DHARMA RESEMBLANCE AGE will last for the same amount of time."

Sutra= T. 21 c 3

At that time, the World Honored One, wishing to restate this principle spoke verses saying,
O Bhikshus, all of you,
Listen with a single mind,
For that which I say
Is true, real, and without error.

Outline:

K2. Verses

L1. Admonishment

to listen.

Commentary:

AT THAT TIME, THE WORLD HONORED ONE, Shakyamuni Buddha, feared that some people hadn't heard him clearly the first time, or else had already forgotten what he said. He used simple verses to restate the principles. WISHING TO RESTATE THIS PRINCIPLE, SPOKE VERSES SAYING,

O, BHIKSHUS, ALL OF YOU/ LISTEN WITH A SINGLE MIND/

Listen to me with one heart, unconfused. Do not strike
up so much false thinking. FOR THAT WHICH I SAY/ IS
TRUE, REAL, AND WITHOUT ERROR/ The Dharma which I speak
is true, real, and not false. It does not change throughout the three periods of time.

Sutra: T. 21c6

Katyayana, shall
With a variety
Of fine and subtle articles
Make offerings to the Buddhas.
After the extinction of those Buddhas
He will build stupas of the seven jewels
And also, with flowers and incense
Make offerings to their sharira.

Outline:

L2. Causal prac-
tice.

Commentary:

KATYAYANA SHALL/ Katyayana, with his unobstructed
eloquence and his first-rate debating skills, WITH A VAR-
IETY/ OF FINE AND SUBTLE ARTICLES/ The finest, most beautiful things, MAKE OFFERINGS TO THE BUDDHAS/

AFTER THE EXTINCTION OF THOSE BUDDHAS/ HE WILL BUILD

STUPAS OF THE SEVEN JEWELS/ AND, ALSO, WITH FLOWERS AND
INCENSE/ MAKE OFFERINGS TO THEIR SHARIRA/

Sutra: T. 21 c9
Jn his final body
He will attain the Buddha wisdom
And realize proper enlightenment.

Outline:

L3. Attaining the
Fruit.

Commentary:

IN HIS FINAL BODY/ HE WILL ATTAIN THE BUDDHA WISDOM/
become a Buddha, AND REALIZE PROPER ENLIGHTENMENT/ accomplishing Anuttarasamyaksambodhi, the unsurpassed enlightenment.

Sutra : T. 21 c10
His country will be pure
And he will cross over limitless
Myriads of millions of beings ;
From the ten directions
He will receive offerings.
His Buddha light
Will be unsurpassed

As a Buddha his name will be
Jambunada Gold Light.
Bodhisattvas, and Sound Hearers
Having severed all existence
Unlimited and innumerable
Will adorn his land.

Outline:

L4. Purity of the
land.

Commentary:

HIS COUNTRY WILL BE PURE/ without any filth, AND HE
WILL CROSS OVER LIMITLESS/ MYRIADS OF MILLIONS OF BEINGS/
FROM THE TEN DIRECTIONS/ HE WILL RECEIVE OFFERINGS/ HIS
BUDDHA LIGHT/ WILL BE UNSURPASSED/ AS A BUDDHA, HIS NAME
WILL BE/ JAMBUNADA GOLD-LIGHT/ BODHISATTVAS AND SOUND
HEARERS/ HAVING SEVERED ALL EXISTENCE/ UNLIMITED AND IM-
MEASURABLE/ WILL ADORN HIS LAND/ having severed the bond
of existence in the desire, form, and formless realms.

Sutra: T. 21 C 15
At that time, the World Honored One,
further spoke to the assembly. "I now tell
you that Mahamaudgalyayana will in the
future, with various articles, make offerings

to eight thousand Buddhas, honoring and
venerating them. After the extinction of
those Buddhas, he will erect for each of them
a stupa one thousand yojanas in height and
five hundred yojanas in breadth, and made
of the seven jewels, gold, silver, lapis lazuli,
mother of pearl, carneilian, pearls, and
agate. He will make offerings to it of many
flowers, beaded necklaces, paste incense,
powdered incense, burning incense, silk
canopies and banners. After that, he will
further make offerings to two hundred
myriads of millions of Buddhas in the
same manner.

Outline:

J3. Prediction for Maha-

maudgalyayana.

K1. Prose.

L1. Causal prac-

tice.

Commentary:

AT THAT TIME, when THE WORLD HONORED ONE, Shakyamuni
Buddha had finished the verses, he decided to bestow a

prediction upon Mahamaudgalyayana. FURTHER SPOKE TO THE ASSEMBLY. "I NOW TELL YOU THAT MAHAMAUDGALYAYANA WILL, IN THE FUTURE," Maudgalyayana means descendant of bean-gatherers." He was foremost in spiritual powers. "WITH VARIOUS ARTICLES, MAKE OFFERINGS TO EIGHT THOUSAND BUD-DHAS, HONORING AND VENERATING THEM. AFTER THE EXTINCTION OF THOSE BUDDHAS, HE WILL ERECT FOR EACH OF THEM A STUPA ONE THOUSAND YOJANAS IN HEIGHT AND FIVE HUNDRED YOJANAS IN BREADTH, AND MADE OF THE SEVEN JEWELS--GOLD, SILVER, LAPIS LAZULI, MOTHER OF PEARL, CARNEILIAN, PEARLS, AND AGATE. HE WILL MAKE OFFERINGS TO IT OF MANY FLOWERS, BEADED NECKLACES, PASTE INCENSE, POWDERED INCENSE, BURN-ING INCENSE, SILK CANOPIES, AND BANNERS. AFTER THAT, HE WILL FURTHER MAKE OFFERINGS TO TWO HUNDRED MYRIADS OF MIL-LIONS OF BUDDHAS IN THE SAME MANNER." So now, when you cultivate, you want to become a Buddha right away! You want to get enlightened right away! And you still haven't gotten rid of your jealousy and contrariness. If you be-came a Buddha now, you would be a jealous and contrary Buddha! No one would make offerings to you. When you cultivate, the first thing is to develop a compassionate mind, a patient, generous, vigorous, concentrated, and wise mind. If you haven't developed your mind in accord with the Six Perfections, how can you expect to become a Buddha? Mahamaudgalyayana will be making offerings to eight thousand Buddhas and then, later, to two hundred myriads of millions of Buddhas.

Sutra: T. 21 C 21

He will then become a Buddha called Tamalapattracandana Fragrance Thus Come One, one worthy of offerings, of proper and universal knowledge, one whose understanding and conduct are complete, a well-gone one who understands the world, an unsurpassed lord, a taming and regulating hero, teacher of gods and humans, Buddha, World Honored One.

Outline:

L2. Attaining

the Fruit.

Commentary:

What is "TAMALAPATTRACANDANA?" Tamalapattra means "worthy one whose nature is without filth." One who has attained the position of a worthy sage has no filth in his self-nature. Candana, called "Ox-head Candana", is a kind of incense that can be smelled at a distance of forty miles. He will be complete with the ten titles of a Buddha.

Time passes quickly. October has gone and November is here. Next Wednesday, five left-home people are going to Taiwan to take the complete precepts of the Great Veicle. It's a historical first. Never before have so many gone from the West to seek the Dharma. Because it is the first time, it is not easy. It is most difficult and entails the most demonic-obstacles. So these five people must be solid, sincere, and persevering. You must be as solid as a diamond, able to destroy all the heavenly demons and outside ways and not be turned by them. You must also be very sincere. You must also persevere. You are bound to run into a lot of demonic-obstacles and demonic tests. If you want to cultivate, demons will certainly come around. They are your indirect helpers. They are afraid that you won't cultivate, so they make sure that you do. There are demons who were even former friends. They may have been your friends, but as soon as they heard that you were going to leave home, they decided to give you a hard time to test you out. If you don't understand what's going on, you're going to think, "Oh, we were such good friends. Why have you turned on me like this?" Actually, they are helping you.

Others run into the demons of sickness. Before they decided to cultivate, they weren't bothered by sickness. As soon as they start cultivating, they get every sickness in the book. Their head is confused, their eyes get blurry, their ears grow deaf, and their teeth start hurting! Sick, sick, sick! Just to see if they can take it. If they can stand it, they'll come to realize that this body is nothing but a stinking bag of skin. What's with all

this pain? There is no pain in the self-nature. In this
way, they will overcome their demonic obstacles.

Others run into the demon of poverty. The more they
cultivate, the poorer they get. Soon they are so poor they
can't afford a pair of socks or a handkerchief! They start
thinking, "What's the good of leaving home? I don't have
any money. I can't buy anything!"

In general, all the various demons attack: wealth demons, sex demons, human demons, ghostly demons, heavenly
demons, earthly demons. But all these demons are not as
harmful as the demon of your own mind. Take care that the
demon of your own mind doesn't get control. It will cause
you to think things like, "Leaving home is really stupid.
It's meaningless. Once you leave home you can't do anything anymore. It's entirely too restrictive."

Take care to remain in control of the situation. You
are going to seek the precepts. When it's time to work,
work. When it's time to study, study. Maintain the awesome deportment like the Bhikshu Ma-sheng, who impressed
Maudgalyayana so much that he, too, wanted to leave home.
Don't bounce around and get upset at every little thing.
When you return, you should have a very special manner.
What is that? You'll find out when you return. Basically, there wan't enough money even to buy your plane
tickets, but I recited a mantra and the money came.

Sutra: T. 21 C 24

His aeon will be called full of joy. His country will be called Delighted Mind. His land will be flat and even with crystal for soil, and jeweled trees for adornments. Real pearl flowers will be scattered about, purifying it entirely, so that those who see it rejoice. There will be many gods, humans, Bodhisattvas and Sound Hearers, limitless and uncountable in number.

Outline:

L3. The aeon and the country.

Commentary:

"When the Venerable Mahamaudgalyayana becomes a Buddha, HIS AEON WILL BE CALLED FULL OF JOY; everyone there will be happy and filled with the happiness of Dharma. All the citizens of that land will delight in the Buddhadharma, and so the land will be called DELIGHTED MIND. HIS LAND WILL BE FLAT AND EVEN. The soil won't be dirt, it will be CRYSTAL. It will have JEWELED TREES FOR ADORNMENTS, trees made of the seven jewels." In our world, there are coral trees. They are made in the ocean by little creatures. I saw them when I went to Thailand. Long

ago in China, there was a very wealthy person. An official invited him to lunch. After lunch, he showed him one
of his coral trees and said, "Do you see this coral tree?
It's incredibly expensive and fine." The person reached
out and grabbed it. It was about two feet tall. Anyway,
he threw it on the ground and smashed it. The official
was very upset, but the man said, "Don't worry, I have
lots. I'll bring you one tomorrow." The next he sent
him one that was three feet tall. Actually, he was just
trying to show off how wealthy he was and make the official think he had all kinds of precious things.

The trees in this Buddhaland were made of the seven
jewels. "REAL PEARL FLOWERS WILL BE SCATTERED ABOUT,
PURIFYING IT ENTIRELY. Flowers made of real pearls will
constantly be falling through space, covering the land.
SO THAT THOSE WHO SEE IT REJOICE. THERE WILL BE MANY GODS,
HUMANS, BODHISATTVAS, AND SOUND HEARERS, LIMITLESS AND UN-
COUNTABLE IN NUMBER." Although the text doesn't say it
specifically, the four evil paths will not exist there,
either.

Sutra: T. 21 c 26
His lifespan as a Buddha will last for twenty-four minor aeons.

Outline:

L4. Lifespan.

Commentary:

"As a Buddha he will live for TWENTY-ONE MINOR AEONS."
Of the four great disciples, he will live the longest as
a Buddha. The others live for twelve minor aeons, so his
lifespan is twice as long.

Sutra : T. 21 c 27
The Proper Dharma will dwell there for
forty minor aeons. The Dharma Resemblance Age will dwell also for forty minor
aeons.

Outline:

> L5. Proper and Re-
> semblance Ages.

Commentary:

"THE PROPER DHARMA age and the DHARMA RESEMBLANCE AGE"
will also last twice as long as that of the other disciples
mentioned.

Sutra: T. 21 c 28
At that time, the World Honored One,
wishing to restate this principle spoke verses,
saying:
My disciple

Great Maudgalyayana
Having cast aside this body
Will view eight thousand
Two hundred myriads of millions
Of Buddhas, World Honored Ones.
And, for the sake of the Buddha Way
Will honor and make offerings to them.
In the presence of those Buddhas,
He will always practice Brahman conduct,
Throughout limitless aeons,
Reverently upholding the Buddhadharma.
After the extinction of those Buddhas,
He will build stupas of the seven jewels,
Displaying golden spires
And with flowers, incense, and instru-
mental music
He will make offerings
To the Buddhas' stupas.

Outline:

K2. Verse.

L1. Causal prac-

tice.

Commentary:

Having finished the prose passage, Shakyamuni Buddha THE WORLD HONORED ONE, wanted to retell the causes and conditions surrounding Mahamaudgalyayana, so he used VERSES and said,

MY DISCIPLE/ The Buddha is obviously very fond of him. GREAT MADGALYAYANA/ HAVING CAST ASIDE THIS BODY/ after he has gotten rid of his present Sound Hearer Body, WILL VIEW EIGHT THOUSAND/ TWO HUNDRED MYRIADS OF MILLIONS/ OF BUDDHAS, WORLD HONORED ONES/ AND, FOR THE SAKE OF THE BUDDHA WAY/ WILL HONOR AND MAKE OFFERINGS TO THEM/

IN THE PRESENCE OF THOSE BUDDHAS/ HE WILL ALWAYS PRACTICE BRAHMAN CONDUCT/ All his conduct will be pure. THROUGHOUT LIMITLESS AEONS/ REVERENTLY UPHOLDING THE BUD-DHADHARMA/ in every life, life after life. AFTER THE EX-TINCTION OF THOSE BUDDHAS/ HE WILL BUILD STUPAS OF THE SEVEN JEWELS/ DISPLAYING GOLDEN SPIRES/ AND WITH FLOWERS, INCENSE, AND INSTRUMENTAL MUSIC/ HE WILL MAKE OFFERINGS/ TO THE BUDDHAS' STUPAS/

Sutra: T. 22 a 7

Gradually, having perfected
The Bodhisattva Path,
In a land called Delighted Intent,
He will become a Buddha
Called Tamala
Candana Fragrance.

Outline:

> L2. Attaining the
> fruit and the name
> of the land.

Commentary:

GRADUALLY, HAVING PERFECTED/ gradually having prac-
ticed THE BODHISATTVA PATH, that is, the Six Perfections
and the Ten Thousand Conducts, IN A LAND CALLED DELIGHTED
INTENT/ HE WILL BECOME A BUDDHA/ CALLED TAMALA/ CANDANA
FRAGRANCE/ "worthy one whose nature is free of filth."
He will emit a fragrance like Candana Ox-head Incense.

Sutra: T. 22 a 9
His lifespan as a Buddha will be Twenty four minor aeons.

Outline:

> L3. Lifespan.

Commentary:

His lifespan is twice that of the other great disciples mentioned.

Sutra: T. 22 a 9
Always, for gods and humans

*He will expound and proclaim the Buddha
Way.
There will be limitless Sound Hearers
In number like the Ganges sands,
With the Three Clarities and Six Pene-
trations
And great, awesome virtue.
There will be uncountable Bodhisattvas
Vigorous and of solid resolve
And who, with regard to the Buddhas'
wisdom
Are irreversible.*

Outline:

L4. Purity of land.

Commentary:

ALWAYS, FOR GODS AND HUMANS/ HE WILL EXPOUND AND PRO-
CLAIM THE BUDDHA WAY/ He will observe the potential of the
beings and speak the Dharma accordingly. He will speak
whatever dharma is necessary in order to cross them over.
He will proclaim the pathway towards the realization of
Buddhahood.

THERE WILL BE LIMITLESS SOUND HEARERS/ IN NUMBER LIKE
THE GANGES SANDS/ WITH THE THREE CLARITIES AND SIX PENE-
TARTIONS/ AND GREAT, AWESOME VIRTUE/

THERE WILL BE UNCOUNTABLE BODHISATTVAS/ VIGOROUS AND
OF SOLID RESOLVE/ AND WHO, WITH REGARD TO THE BUDDHA'S
WISDOM/ ARE IRREVERSIBLE/ They will have obtained the three
kinds of irreversibility: irreversibility of position, irreversibility of thought, and irreversibility of conduct.

Sutra: T. 22 a 13

After that Buddha's extinction
The Proper Dharma will dwell
For forty minor aeons,
And the Dharma Resemblance Age will
be the same.

Outline:

L5. Proper and

Image Ages.

Commentary:

AFTER THAT BUDDHA'S EXTINCTION/ after he has entered
Nirvana, THE PROPER DHARMA WILL DWELL/ in the world FOR
FORTY MINOR AEONS/ AND THE DHARMA RESEMBLANCE AGE WILL
BE THE SAME/ as the Proper Dharma Age.

Now, having given this prediction concerning Mahamaudgalyayana, the Buddha saw that his other disciples
had grown nervous, wondering when they would get predictions. Did they have a chance to become Buddhas? So he
gives them all predictions here.

Sutra: T. 22 a 14

All my disciples
Having perfected their awesome virtue,
All five hundred of them
Shall be given predictions
And in a future age
Will become Buddhas.
Of my own and your former
Causes and conditions
I now will tell :
All of you, listen well!

Outline:

> G2. Speaking of former lives for
> those of inferior dispositions.

Commentary:

ALL MY DISCIPLES/ HAVING PERFECTED THEIR AWESOME VIR-
TUE/ ALL FIVE HUNDRED OF THEM/ SHALL BE GIVEN PREDICTIONS/
AND IN A FUTURE AGE/ WILL BECOME BUDDHAS/

OF MY OWN AND YOUR FORMER/ CAUSES AND CONDITIONS/
From former lives we have causal affinities in common, and
so we meet here in this Dharma assembly, and I speak the
Dharma for you. In the future, you shall receive your
predictions of Buddhahood and become Buddhas. Were it
not for these causal affinities, even though the Buddha

spoke the Dharma, you would not be able to come and listen.

We are all presently gathered in this <u>Dharma</u> <u>Flower</u> <u>Sutra</u> Assembly because of causal conditions from former lives. If it were not for that causal affinity, we would not have met here. I NOW WILL TELL:/ ALL OF YOU, LISTEN WELL!/ Pay attention. Like right now, I am lecturing <u>The</u> <u>Dharma</u> <u>Flower</u> <u>Sutra</u> for you and you should listen. The situation is the same. You should all listen well. Shakyamuni Buddha spoke the Dharma on Vulture Peak. We didn't have the opportunity to hear it right then. Now, however, we can look at the portraits of all the Patriarchs. You shouldn't look at the pictures of Han-shan and Shih-te and think they are so funny looking. They are Bodhisattvas who deliberately manifested that special style. So, as you meet each patriarch, they will meet you. You will recognize one another because of former causes and conditions.

Speaking of pictures, I remember that when I was in Hong Kong there was a young child who had heart disease. The doctor told him he had to stay in bed and sleep for five years, without getting out of bed. Somehow, he got hold of my biography and saw my picture in it. For some strange reason, he pulled up in full lotus, placed the picture in front of him, put his palms together and began to recite my name. Everyone else in the house would recite Namo Amitabha Buddha, but he recited my name! He re-

cited this way, morning to night, for seventy days. Then
he saw me come out of the picture and rub him on the head.
After that, his heart disease was cured.

***

Index

***

A BRIGHT STAR IN A TROUBLED WORLD:

THE CITY OF TEN THOUSAND BUDDHAS

Located at Talmage, California, just south of Ukiah and about two hours north of San Francisco, is Wonderful Enlightenment Mountain. Situated at the base is the 237 acre area holding 60 buildings which is called the City of Ten Thousand Buddhas which is fast becoming a center for religious, educational, and social programs for world Buddhism.

At present, the complex houses Tathagata Monastery and the Great Compassion House for men, Great Joyous Giving House for women, the campus of Dharma Realm Buddhist University, and a large auditorium. Plans are underway to present many kinds of programs to benefit people in spirit, mind, and body--a home for the aged, a hospital emphasizing the utilization of both eastern and western healing techniques, an alternative mental health facility, and educational programs ranging from pre-school through Ph.D. Cottage industries, organic farming, and living in harmony with our environment will be stressed. The City is an ideal spot for conventions where people of all races and religions can exchange their ideas and unite their energies to

Buddha-recitation at the City of Ten Thousand Buddhas

V.

A Dharma lecture in the Hall of Ten Thousand Buddhas

promote human welfare and world peace.
Religious cultivation will be foremost and the City will be instrumental in the transmission of the orthodox precepts of the Buddhas, thus developing Bhikshus and Bhikshunis to teach and maintain the Buddhadharma. Rigorous cultivation sessions are held regularly and the grounds of the monastery provide a pure and quiet setting to pursue the study of meditation. A number of facilities are available for those found qualified to retreat into contemplative seclusion. The spacious grounds have more than a hundred acres of pine groves, and a running stream.

At a time when the world is torn with strife, the City of Ten Thousand Buddhas appears as a guiding star for all of us to discover life's true meaning and pass it on to future generations.

The four-fold assembly of disciples: City of Ten Thousand Buddhas

VI.

DHARMA REALM BUDDHIST UNIVERSITY

A SPECIAL APPROACH

Focus on Values: examining the moral foundations of ancient spiritual traditions, relating those traditions to space-age living, and finding what it takes to live in harmony with our social and natural environments.

Focus on change: a key to understanding ourselves, our relationships, and the crises of the modern world. What we seek is to be open to new ways of seeing ourselves, to new modes of relating to friend and stranger, and to new methods and technological aids that supplement and open up for us the limitless store of human wisdom, past and present.

Total environment education where teacher and student are partners in the educational process and share responsibility for it. Learning takes place both in and out of the classroom in a community which is concerned with the complex problems of society.

Personally tailored programs in which education need not be constricted by traditional department boundries. The emphasis will be on meaningful learning, not just the accumulation of facts and test-taking skills.

Education for young and old where the different generations come together to share in the experience of learning and thereby enrich that experience. The University also especially encourages those with valuable life experience to apply for special experimental learning credits.

GUIDING IDEALS

These are the ideals which will guide education at Dharma Realm University:

To explain and share the Buddha's teaching;
To develop straightforward minds and hearts;
To benefit society;
To encourage all beings to seek enlightenment.

CAMPUS

The main campus of Dharma Realm University is located at the foot of Cow Mountain National Recreation Area in the beautiful Ukiah valley. It is surrounded by the woods, meadows, and farmland of the City of Ten Thousand Buddhas. The University will be housed in several large buildings set among trees and broad lawns. One classroom building has been newly refurbished for educational use. The air is clean and fresh, and the climate is pleasant and temperate (av. min. temp. 43.2 deg; av. max. temp. 76 deg.) Rarely falling below freezing in the winter and usually dry in the summer, the area is very fertile with much grape and fruit tree cultivation. Close by are the Russian River, Lake Mendocino and Clear Lake, several hot springs, redwood and other national forest lands, and the scenic Pacific Coast.

PROGRAMS-Undergraduate and graduate, full-time and part-time

The University intends to provide quality education in a number of fields, with   emphasis (wherever possible) on matching classroom theory with practical experience. The curriculum is divided into three main areas:

The Letters and Science Program: In addition to a regular curriculum of Humanities, Social, and Natural Sciences, special emphasis will be laid on East-West studies, with strong offerings in Asian languages, literature, philosophy, and religion. We expect pioneering interdisciplinary approaches in many of these areas, combining the best of Asian and Western approaches to education. Education for personal growth and the development of special competencies will be the twin aims of the program.

The Buddhist Studies Program will emphasize a combination of traditional and modern methods including actual practice of the Buddhadharma as well as scholarly investigation. Offerings will range from introductory fundamentals to advanced meditation and will include advanced seminars in both English and canonical languages.

The Arts Program: Practical Arts will concentrate on putting knowledge to work right away in workshops for building a living community ecology, energy, gardening and nutrition, community planning, management, etc. Creative Arts offerings will include the meeting of East and West in a whole panorama of studio arts. There will be special courses in Chinese calligraphy, in the creation of Buddha images, and in music. Individual Arts workshops will include t'ai-chi ch'üan, yoga, meditational techniques, wilderness survival, and much more.

THE INTERNATIONAL TRANSLATION CENTER

The Translation Center will sponsor courses, workshops, and special programs concerned with translation techniques for a wide range of languages and will coordinate a unique degree program in translation.

THE WORLD RELIGIONS CENTER

The World Religions Center will sponsor workshops, conferences, and other special programs to aid in mutual understanding and good will among those of different faiths.

SPECIAL INTERNATIONAL STUDENT PROGRAM

In the future, there will be special emphasis on welcoming students from Asian countries to complement the University's strong offerings in East-West studies. Areas of special interest to Asian students will be added to the curriculum as well as a strong English as a Second Language (ESL) Program.

DONATIONS

Dharma Realm University welcomes your help with donations. In addition to financial assistance, the University needs home and office furniture, books and scholarly journals, supplies and equipment, and the services of volunteers. *All donations are tax deductable.*

VERSE ON RETURNING THE LIGHT

Truly recognize your own faults
And don't discuss the faults of others.
Other's faults are just your own faults,
Being one with everyone
is called great compassion.

— Ven. Master Hsuan Hua

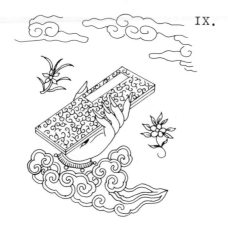

THE BUDDHIST TEXT TRANSLATION SOCIETY

Chairperson: The Venerable Tripitaka Master Hsüan Hua
               Abbot of Gold Mountain Monastery and
               Tathagata Monastery.
               Chancellor of Dharma Realm Buddhist
               University.
               Professor of the Tripitaka and
               the Dhyanas

PRIMARY TRANSLATING COMMITTEE:

Chairpersons: Bhikshuni Heng Yin
               Bhikshuni Heng Ch'ih

Members: Bhikshu Heng Kuan
           Bhikshu Heng K'ung
           Bhikshu Heng Sure
           Bhikshu Heng Shun
           Bhikshu Heng Tso
           Bhikshuni Heng Hsien
           Bhikshuni Heng Ch'ing
           Bhikshuni Heng Hua
           Bhikshuni Heng Chen
           Bhikshuni Heng Ming
           Bhikshuni Heng Tao
           Bhikshu Heng Teng
           Bhikshu Heng Ch'i
           Bhikshu Heng Kung

       Upasaka Kuo Jung (R.B.) Epstein
       Upasika Kuo Ts'an (Terri) Nicholson
       Upasaka Kuo Chou (David) Rounds
       Upasaka Chou Kuo Li
       Professor Hsing Tsun Lee
       Professor Wu-yi

REVIEWING COMMITTEE:

Chairpersons: Bhikshu Heng Tso
                 Upasaka Kuo Jung (R.B.) Epstein

Members: Bhikshu Heng Kuan
                 Bhikshu Heng Sure
                 Bhikshu Heng Teng
                 Bhikshu Heng Ch'i
                 Bhikshu Heng Kung
                 Bhikshuni Heng Yin
                 Bhikshuni Heng Ch'ih
                 Bhikshuni Heng Hsien
                 Bhikshuni Heng Ch'ing
                 Bhikshuni Heng Hua
                 Bhikshuni Heng Chen
                 Bhikshuni Heng Tao

Upasaka Kuo Jung (R.B.) Epstein
Upasika Hsieh Ping-ying
Upasika Kuo Ts'an Nicholson
Upasika Phuong Kuo Wu
Upasika Kuo Chin Vickers
Upasika Kuo Han Epstein
Upasaka Kuo Chou Rounds
Upasaka Chou Kuo Li
Professor Hsing Tsun Lee
Professor Wu-yi

EDITING COMMITTEE:

Chairperson: Bhikshu Heng Kuan

Members: Bhikshu Heng K'ung
                 Bhikshu Heng Sure
                 Bhikshu Heng Lai
                 Bhikshu Heng Shun
                 Bhikshu Heng Ch'au
                 Bhikshu Heng Ch'i
                 Bhikshuni Heng Yin
                 Bhikshuni Heng Ch'ih
                 Bhikshuni Heng Hsien
                 Bhikshuni Heng Ch'ing
                 Bhikshuni Heng Chu
                 Bhikshuni Heng Hua
                 Bhikshuni Heng Chen
                 Bhikshuni Heng Jieh
                 Bhikshuni Heng Ming
                 Bhikshuni Heng Tao

EDITING COMMITTEE, continued

Upasaka Kuo Jung (R.B.) Epstein
Upasaka Kuo Tsun (Randy) Dinwiddie
Upasika Kuo Shun Nolan
Upasika Kuo Chin (Janet) Vickers
Upasaka Kuo Ts'an Nicholson
Upasaka Kuo Chou (David) Rounds
Upasika Kuo Lin (Nancy) Lethcoe
Upasaka Chou Kuo Li
Professor Hsing Tsun Lee
Professor Wu-yi
Professor Yu Kuo K'ung

CERTIFYING COMMITTEE:

Chairperson: *Venerable Tripitaka Master Hsüan Hua*

Members: Bhikshu Heng Kuan
               Bhikshu Heng Sure
               Bhikshu Heng Tso
               Bhikshuni Heng Yin
               Bhikshuni Heng Ch'ih
               Bhikshuni Heng Hsien
               Bhikshuni Heng Ch'ing
               Bhikshuni Heng Tao

Upasaka Wong Kuo-chun   Transcribers: Bhikshuni
Upasaka Kuo Jung Epstein   Heng-chai, Bhikshuni Heng-
Upasika T'an Kuo Shih   wen, Upasika Kuo-li
Upasika Kuo Chin Vickers

BUDDHIST TEXT TRANSLATION SOCIETY
EIGHT REGULATIONS

A translator must free himself or herself from the motives of
personal fame and reputation.
A translator must cultivate an attitude free from arrogance
and conceit.
A translator must refrain from aggrandizing himself or herself
and denigrating others.
A translator must not establish himself or herself as the
standard of correctness and suppress the work of others with
his or her faultfinding.
A translator must take the Buddha-mind as his or her own mind.
A transaltor must use the wisdom of the Selective Dharma Eye
to determine true principles.
A translator must request the Elder Virtuous Ones of the ten
directions to certify his or her translations.
A translator must endeavor to propagate the teachings by
printing sutras, shastra texts,and vinaya texts when the
translations are certified as being correct.

XII.

PUBLICATIONS FROM THE BUDDHIST TEXT TRANSLATION SOCIETY

THE FLOWER ADORNMENT SUTRA is known as the king of kings
among Buddhist Sutras because of its great length (81 rolls
of over 700,000 Chinese characters) and its extreme profundity, containing the most complete explanation of the Buddha's
state and the spiritual path to enlightenment. The Buddhist
Text Translation Society is presently working on translations
of the entire text of this Sutra accompanied by the exten-
sive interlinear commentary of the Venerable Tripitaka Master
Hsüan Hua. The entire translation work including the Preface
and Prologue of National Master Ch'ing Liang as well as the
39 Chapters of the Sutra is expected to be more than 150
volumes when completed.

> *FLOWER ADORNMENT SUTRA PREFACE*-a bilingual publication
> containing the brilliant verse preface to the *Avatamsaka
> Sutra* composed by National Master Ch'ing Liang. The inter-
> linear commentary by Tripitaka Master Hua elucidates
> the verse with clarity based in the oral tradition of
> Orthodox Buddhism and directed to modern students of
> the Way. softbound, 218 pages. NOW AVAILABLE.

> *THE TEN GROUNDS CHAPTER OF THE FLOWER ADORNMENT SUTRA*.
> Volume I contains the First Ground, that of Happiness,
> and discusses the Bodhisattva's conduct of giving
> and clarifies the quality of being unmoving. This
> bi-lingual publication will be available SPRING, 1980.

> *FLOWER ADORNMENT SUTRA PROLOGUE, VOLUME ONE*. In this
> masterful work National Master Ch'ing Liang elucidates
> the first nine doors of the Hsien Shou's Ten Doors
> of Discrimination. This publication will also be bi-
> lingual. Volume One begins the Doors. AVAILABLE SPRING
> 1980.

THE WONDERFUL DHARMA LOTUS FLOWER SUTRA is the sutra for
accomplishing Buddhahood. In it, the Buddha opens the provisional to reveal the actual teaching. He sets forth the
One Buddha Vehicle; all beings possess the Buddha nature
and are destined for Buddhahood. Although we are all potential Buddhas, it is only through cultivation and practice of
the principles of the Buddhadharma that we can actualize
that potential. Therefore, the commentary of the Venerable
Master is filled with analogies, examples, expedients, and
exhortations, all for the purpose of leading us to Buddhahood. Found here is the Dharma of the heart, the Dharma
which is aimed only at showing us how to break our attach-
ments and gain liberation. The Buddha's teaching now blooms,
lotus-like,in the West. It is up to us to study and

practice it, and quickly bear the Bodhi-fruit!

DHARMA FLOWER SUTRA, VOL 1. This volume discusses
the Five Periods and the Eight Teachings of the T'ien
T'ai School and then analizes the School's Five Profound Meanings as they relate to the *LOTUS SUTRA.*
Finally, Tripitaka Master Kumarajiva, who translated
the Sutra from Sanskrit to Chinese, is introduced.
Softbound, 66 pages. NOW AVAILABLE.

DHARMA FLOWER SUTRA, VOL 2. Chapter One is explained
in full in this volume and further clarified by the
complete outline of Ming Dynasty Master Ngou-i. In
Chapter One the stage is set for the Buddha's speaking of the Sutra. On Vulture Peak, near the City of
the House of Kings, Shakyamuni Buddha has gathered
with a great assembly of Bhikshus, Arhats, Bodhisattvas,
and the gods and dragons and the eight-fold division.
He manifests six portents and the Bodhisattva Maitreya
asks the Bodhisattva Manjushri to explain the reason
for them. Manjushri Bodhisattva explains in detail,
comparing the present portents to those he saw in the
distant past, in the Dharma assembly of Sun-Moon-Lamp
Buddha. After manifesting the portents, that Buddha
spoke THE WONDERFUL DHARMA LOTUS FLOWER SUTRA. Thus,
the Bodhisattva Manjushri concludes that Shakyamuni
Buddha is about to speak THE DHARMA FLOWER SUTRA as
well. The Venerable Master's commentary provides a
wealth of information on the lives of the Buddha's disciples as well as detailed explanations of terms and
concepts basic to an understanding of the Buddhadharma.
Softbound, 289 pages. NOW AVAILABLE.

DHARMA FLOWER SUTRA, VOL 3. This volume contains
Chapter Two, Expedient Devices. The Buddha emerges
from samadhi to praise the profundity of the Buddhas'
wisdom which is beyond the understanding of both the
Sound Hearers and the Conditioned-Enlightened Ones.
When he praises the Buddhas' use of expedients, many
in the assembly give rise to doubts and so the Buddha
does not wish to explain further. The Venerable
Shariputra requests the Buddha to explain three times
before the Buddha finally consents to continue speaking.
At that point, five thousand in the assembly get up and
leave.   They are not ready to hear the final, perfect
teaching of the *LOTUS SUTRA.* Those who remain, like
the grain after the wind has driven away the chaff,
learn of the One Buddha Vehicle and the fact that
Buddhas appear in the world for the sake of the One

Great Matter: to open and demonstrate, to lead us to awaken and enter, the Buddhas' knowledge and vision, which is just the knowledge and vision of our own true minds. Softbound, 166 pages. NOW AVAILABLE.

DHARMA FLOWER SUTRA, VOL 4. In this volume, Chapter Three, A Parable, is explained. Here, the Buddha is speaking for those of average and inferior roots, who are thus lead to understanding. It is one of the most important chapters in the Sutra and for this reason, the Venerable Tripitaka Master Hua commented on it at length and in great detail.

In the analogy, there is a great elder who left his children at home and went on a journey. As he was returning, he saw that his house had caught fire. He called to the children to come out, but they were so absorbed in their play that they paid no attention to him. The elder then used an expedient device. "Come out," he said. "I have some fine toys for you right outside the door. I have sheep carts, deer carts, and an ox carts. Come out and take them!" Hearing this, the children ran from the house to safety and demanded the carts. Instead of the three cards he had promised, he gave them each a great white ox cart, wonderful far beyond their original hopes.

The great elder is, of course , the Buddha. His children are those of the Three Vehicles and also all living beings. Playing in the burning house of the three realms, living beings continue to amuse themselves, ignoring the Buddha's warnings and unaware of the danger. The Buddha expediently offers the teachings of the Three Vehicles, but gives us instead the One Buddha Vehicle, the Great White Ox Cart. Softbound, 343 pages. NOW AVAILABLE.

DHARMA FLOWER SUTRA, VOL 5. This volume contains Chapter Four, Belief and Understanding. The Sutra Text is written in calligraphy and the volume is illustrated with woodcuts. AVAILABLE FEBRUARY, 1980.

EXPLICACION GENERAL DEL SUTRA EN QUE EL BUDA HABLA DE AMITABHA por Maestro de Tripitaka Hua. Spanish translation of the *Amitabha Sutra*, softbound, 150 pages. NOW AVAILABLE.

THE VAJRA SUTRA, paperbound, 192 pages.
THE DHARANI SUTRA, paperbound, 352 pages.
THE SUTRA OF THE PAST VOWS OF EARTH STORE BODHISATTVA,
hardcover and paperbound, 235 pages.
THE SIXTH PATRIARCH'S DHARMA JEWEL PLATFORM SUTRA, hardcover
and paperbound, 380 pages.
THE SUTRA IN FORTY-TWO SECTIONS, paperbound, 94 pages.
THE AMITABHA SUTRA, paperbound, 204 pages.
THE SHRAMANERA VINAYA AND RULES OF DEPORTMENT, paperbound,
112 pages.

*WITH ONE HEART BOWING TO THE CITY OF TEN THOUSAND BUDDHAS,
VOLUMES 1,2,3.* Dharma Master Heng Ch'au notes: "Teach
and transform with your practice and example, not your mouth.
Live, breathe, and embody the teachings. You can't talk
your way to enlightenment. When the mouth opens the eyes
close." Dharma Master Heng Sure writes: "The wisdom of
the Buddhas is undifferentiated contemplation of all dharmas.
The Buddha sees that all conditioned things are empty. They
do not last and he does not confuse them with himself. Empty,
impermanent, and not self--seeing the world this way, what
can you do? What is left to do? One can only follow pure
principles as taught by the enlightened masters of the past
and present and try your best all the time to save all beings
from their suffering. On a more basic level one should do
all that is good, avoid doing anything that is evil and cultivate the practices that purify the body and mind." The
monks' bowing journey continues at least until the EARTH STORE
BODHISATTVA FESTIVAL held in July, 1980, at the City of Ten
Thousand Buddhas. These paperbound volumes are NOW AVAILABLE.

OPEN YOUR EYES, TAKE A LOOK AT THE WORLD. Records of the
1978 Asia-region visit by the Venerable Master and members
of the   American Buddhist Association. In Penang the
Venerable Master said: "The Buddha said, 'All living beings
have the Buddhanature, all can become Buddhas.' Hence, even
if a living being does not believe in the Buddha, he still
has an inherent Buddhanature, so how can we exclude him
from Buddhism? Unless one can run outside of empty space
and the Dharma realm, one cannot run outside of Buddhism.
Whether he believes or not is just a matter of time. If you
do not believe in Buddhism this life, I'll wait for you
until your next life, and on and on--even for measureless
kalpas--I will still wait for you.
    "If we expand the measure of our hearts, then all
human beings can unite and benefit the world. For the rise
and fall of a country, every person bears a responsibility.

As for the rise and fall of Buddhism, every Buddhist disciple should take it as his or her own responsibility, too. Do not bow to the Buddhas merely out of greed for wealth and fame; rather offer up good conduct and be a true disciple." Softbound, 232 pages.

SONGS FOR AWAKENING. Introducing this volume of words and music to over forty songs which tell of the Buddhadharma, is this verse by the Venerable Master Hua:

> In this reagion the substance of the teaching
>   is in sound,
> These songs and praises wonderfully penetrate
>   the spiritual realm.
> Gandharvas inhale the incense
>   and arrive,
> Kinnaras hear the music
>   and descend.
> Creatures with conditions
>   all are saved,
> Dried up plants and trees
>   come alive again!
> All perfect the wisdom
>   of all modes,
> And together realize Bodhi,
>   the great and honored awakening.

Softbound, 88 pages. Contains drawings, woodcuts, photographs and is indexed according to title and first line. Perfect as a gift to introduce people to the unsurpassed teaching with gentle persuasion, irresistible candor, and heart-felt joy.   NOW AVAILABLE.

VAJRA BODHI SEA, A Monthly Journal of Orthodox Buddhism. This bi-lingual periodical is in its tenth year of publication. Each month a Patriarch is featured as well as a a biography of a contemporary Sanghan and member of the lay community. Sutras with their interlineary commentaries, translations of Shastras and Vinaya material, essays, articles, poems, and stories on Buddhist topics appear regularly. Photographs, woodcuts and line drawings enhance each issue. News From the Dharmarealm keeps one current with Buddhist events East and West and calendars of holidays, notice of important Dharma assemblies, and letters from readers add current import. Yearly subscriptions: $22.00. Three years for $60.00. Single issues: $2.00.   Write to Gold Mountain Monastery, 1731-15th Street, San Francisco, Ca. 94103.

THE SHURANGAMA SUTRA, VOL 1 & 2. paperbound.
PURE LAND AND CH'AN DHARMA TALKS, paperbound 72 pages.
BUDDHA ROOT FARM (Amitabha Buddha Recitation Session), paper-
bound, 72 pages.
RECORDS OF THE LIFE OF THE VENERABLE MASTER HSÜAN HUA, VOL 1
papergound, 96 pages.
RECORDS OF THE LIFE OF THE VENERABLE MASTER HSÜAN HUA, VOL 2
paperbound, 229 pages.
WORLD PEACE GATHERING, paperbound, 128 pages.
THE TEN DHARMA REALMS ARE NOT BEYOND A SINGLE THOUGHT,
verses and explanation, paperbound, 72 pages.
CELEBRISI'S JOURNEY, a novel, paperbound, 178 pages.
LISTEN TO YOURSELF, THINK EVERYTHING OVER (Kuan Yin Bodhi-
sattva Recitation Session and Ch'an Sessions) paperbound.
A GENERAL INTRODUCTION TO THE SINO-AMERICAN BUDDHIST
ASSOCIATION. paperbound 22 pages.

* *

MEMBERSHIP IN THE SINO-AMERICAN BUDDHIST ASSOCIATION

MEMBERSHIP ENTITLES YOU TO: voting rights in the Association,
including the right to cast ballots for the Board of Dir-
ectors, and to qualify to serve on the Board.
                              -membership at Gold Mountain Mon-
astery and the City of Ten Thousand Buddhas.
                              -free attendance at Sutra lectures,
ceremonies, holiday celebrations, and many other events of
the Association.
                              -purchase of any of the Associa-
tion's publications at half price.
                              -attendance at meditation and
recitation sessions, including meals, lodging, and instruc-
tion, at half price.
                              -a free subscription to VAJRA
BODHI SEA, the journal of the Association.
                              -a membership card, registration
on the Association's membership roll, and for term and
life members, a special membership pin.